Biocultural Interactions
and Human Variation

ELEMENTS OF ANTHROPOLOGY
A Series of Introductions

Biocultural Interactions and Human Variation

Jane H. Underwood

University of Arizona

WM. C. BROWN COMPANY PUBLISHERS
Dubuque, Iowa

ANTHROPOLOGY SERIES

Consulting Editors

Frank Johnston
University of Pennsylvania

Henry Selby
Temple University

For Jack Goins

Contents

Preface

The uniqueness, and the strength, of anthropology derives from its holistic and eclectic approach to the study of mankind. We are all organic beings, belonging to the animal world, yet peculiar among living forms because we are, above all, cultural beings. Appropriately, anthropologists have focused on the biological *and* cultural dimensions of human life. This perspective expresses the compositionist viewpoint which attempts to understand human diversity through inferences based on the study of function, integration, and processes operating at the biochemical, organismic, and population levels.

While the meaning of human variation can appropriately be studied at each of these levels, a comprehensive view of the maintenance and patterning of human diversity must ultimately relate to the population level. In terms of modern theory, evolution may be defined as changes in allele frequencies of populations through time. The differences we observe in living populations are the results of evolutionary processes operating in the past and at present. This book attempts to review the complex nexus of cultural and biological influences affecting the biological diversity of human populations. Fundamental principles of Mendelian and population genetics are briefly reviewed and followed by a summary of the implications of differences in diet, disease history, demography, and mating structure on the genetic composition of human populations. The purpose, throughout, is to sensitize the reader to the significance, even the essentiality, of human diversity to our continuing existence and evolution.

It would be impossible here to appropriately acknowledge all those who contributed so greatly to the writing of this text. To all those students who have taught me so much, I offer my special gratitude.

1 | Introduction

Although our concern with human variation has roots extending even beyond the earliest pages of recorded history, the written records of this interest suggest the pervasiveness of Man's attention to similarities and differences among human beings. Chinese writers of the Han Dynasty (ca. 200 B.C.) described the "yellow-haired, green-eyed barbarians" of distant lands and disparagingly ascribed the origins of divergent peoples in remote provinces to the union of human and animal. The ancient Egyptians were wont, on occasion, to burn red-haired men and to scatter their ashes over crop fields to ensure the fertility of the earth, while archaic Vedic rites in India recommended the sacrifice of a black victim to procure rain. Hanno, a Carthaginian navigator of the pre-Christian era, had scant opportunity to examine three female "hairy savages" (probably gorillas, according to later writers), captured on the western coast of Africa, for all three victims quickly escaped. Herodotus (484-425 B.C.), despite his personal examination of Persian and Egyptian skulls, seemed at least somewhat credulous in his quick acceptance of a prevailing explanation for the purportedly greater thickness of Egyptian skulls: "The Egyptians, they said, from early childhood have the head shaved, and so by the action of the sun the skull becomes thick and hard."[1]

As European explorers sailed ever further, and travelers' journals continued to record the discovery of hitherto unknown groups, prevailing notions of the range of human variation seemed limited only by the boundaries of geographic ventures and the imaginative constraints of creative writers. Even judicious observers would occasionally include hearsay reports of dubious veracity. Antonio Pigafetta, a somewhat laconic journalist of the Magellan expedition, reported an old pilot's tale of an island where tiny people had ears so long that they wrapped themselves in them!

Expectably, attempts to explain the diversity of mankind were often as ingenuous as travelers' reports were inventive. Leonardo da Vinci argued that natives of hot regimes acquired their dark skin color from their habit of working during the cooler nights, while inhabitants of cooler climes became fair from their propensity for working during the warmer daytime. Many other writers of the same period saw in human differences the consequences of Divine judgment applied to the several ancestors of different living human groups. In the light of greater knowledge and familiarity with numerous human populations, the extent and limitations of human

1. Manuel Komroff, ed., *The History of Herodotus*, trans. C. Rawlinson (New York: Tudor Publishing Company, 1943), p. 149.

variation are more accurately known today.

Unlike earlier observers, we can say with certainty that there are no green-skinned people on this planet nor any who exceed ten feet in stature. Rather, the distribution of skin color, head form, stature, and many other visible traits has been studied in many parts of the world, and the degree of variation, as well as the limited extent of such differences, has been fairly well documented. Moreover, extensive investigations of the distribution of many biochemical traits, such as blood group antigens, hemoglobin variants, and red cell enzyme systems, have been made in many human populations and some notion of the range of human biochemical variation is indicated by the brief summary of the distribution of the ABO blood groups in selected populations around the world presented in Table 1.

The conclusions to be drawn from the information now available are rather straightforward. There are few *phenotypic traits* (detectable expressions of the genetic composition of the individual) known in man on which any single group of humans holds a monopoly. Dark skin color, for example, is found among many natives of sub-Saharan countries, but within any such African group, individuals vary within a limited range as to the extent of dark pigmentation, some appearing lighter than others. However, certain populations in Melanesia also show a range of variation in skin color closely parallel to that found in some African groups. Among Southeast Asians, the distribution of skin color in certain populations is such that many individuals would be found with lighter pigmentation than could be found among either Melanesians or sub-Saharan blacks, yet some of the Southeast Asians would be as darkly pigmented as some members of either the African or Melanesian populations.

Other visible traits show different distributions, so that no simple classification can encompass the range of human variation in a meaningful manner. Thus, in parts of Africa, groups such as the Pygmy and Bantu Negro, while similar in the range and distribution of skin color variation, may differ greatly in the statistical average and coefficient of variability for stature, while the Andamanese Islanders might appear more similar to the African Pygmies in stature than to many of the populations of India to which they are in closer geographic proximity.

When such biochemical traits as the ABO blood group antigens are considered, it becomes clear that most human populations differ from each other in the relative frequencies of such traits rather than in any absolute manner. The blood group type A is present in Africans, Melanesians, Southeast Asians, Europeans, and some American Indian populations, but at differing frequencies. Blood group type O, which is the only blood group found in some unmixed American Indian populations, is also found in Africans, Melanesians, Southeast Asians, and Europeans! In brief, mankind comprises a polymorphic, polytypic species; that is, human populations express considerable intrapopulation, or individual, variability (*phenotypic polymorphism*), while populations within the species differ from one another in the range and distribution of variation for many phenotypic traits (*polytypism*).

While efforts continue to collect additional data on the diversity within and among human populations, attention is increasingly directed to identifying and studying the processes and interactions responsible for the creation and maintenance of variation in human populations. Every human being begins life as a single cell, the *zygote*, or fertilized egg cell, which, through differentiation, growth and development, is born and continues to grow as a unique individual. The core of

TABLE 1

SUMMARY OF ABO BLOOD GROUP PHENOTYPE FREQUENCIES
OF SELECTED POPULATIONS
(prepared by R. Hagaman from Mourant, 1958).

POPULATION	Phenotype			Frequencies		Allele	
	O	A	B	AB	p	q	r
EUROPE							
United Kingdom	.4668	.4172	.0856	.0304	.2568	.0598	.6834
Sweden	.3823	.4736	.0982	.0459	.3063	.0749	.6188
Basques	.5797	.3837	.0271	.0097	.2210	.0186	.7604
Lapps	.2896	.6262	.0446	.0396	.4213	.0429	.5358
Poland	.3299	.3851	.2022	.0828	.2707	.1545	.5748
U.S.S.R. (Russians)	.3330	.3740	.2280	.0650	.2530	.1600	.5870
Germany	.3881	.4351	.1225	.0543	.2853	.0927	.6220
Spain	.4140	.4676	.0881	.0303	.2920	.0612	.6468
Greece	.4348	.3864	.1306	.0481	.2480	.0937	.6583
France	.4270	.4701	.0724	.0305	.2934	.0528	.6538
Italy	.4200	.4340	.1060	.0400	.2750	.0760	.6490
Hungary	.3527	.4052	.1789	.0632	.2717	.1298	.5985
Denmark	.4058	.4404	.1088	.0450	.2826	.0801	.6373
AFRICA							
Egypt	.3264	.3554	.2437	.0745	.2461	.1751	.5788
Morocco (Arabs)	.4236	.2882	.2267	.0615	.1935	.1562	.6503
Ashanti (Ghana)	.5133	.2301	.2124	.0442	.1479	.1376	.7145
Nuer (Sudan)	.5200	.2800	.1700	.0300	.1696	.1058	.7246
Efe Pygmies (Belgian Congo)	.2699	.3586	.2827	.0887	.2587	.2089	.5324
Masai (Denya)	.4807	.2017	.3047	.0129	.1148	.1756	.7096
Bushmen (S.W. Africa)	.5605	.3386	.0852	.0157	.1967	.0519	.7514
Zulu (S. Africa)	.5180	.2460	.2160	.0200	.1441	.1266	.7293
Swazi (S. Africa)	.6160	.1980	.1740	.0120	.1115	.0981	.7904
Yoruba (Nigerian)	.5096	.2274	.2192	.0438	.1462	.1414	.7124
ASIA							
Yemenite Arabs	.5570	.3228	.1076	.0126	.1854	.0622	.7524
Bedouins (Iraq)	.4083	.2663	.2574	.0680	.1843	.1789	.6368

TABLE 1—continued

	O	A	B	AB	p	q	r
Turkey (Asia Minor)	.3246	.4071	.1858	.0825	.2856	.1446	.5698
Hindus (Calcutta)	.3237	.2407	.3624	.0731	.1726	.2500	.5774
Toda (S. India)	.2950	.1950	.3800	.1300	.1765	.2968	.5267
Punjabi (W. Pak.)	.3064	.2448	.3478	.1000	.1910	.2573	.5517
Siamese (Thailand)	.3727	.2184	.3305	.0783	.1612	.2309	.6079
Negritos (Malaya)	.5911	.2453	.1450	.0196	.1423	.0856	.7721
Filipinos	.4490	.2567	.2435	.0507	.1680	.1601	.6719
Macassar (Celebes)	.2872	.2974	.3077	.1077	.2287	.2354	.5359
Ainu (Japan)	.2571	.2813	.3439	.1177	.2249	.2665	.5086
Japanese	.3123	.3917	.2085	.0874	.2786	.1611	.5603
Korea	.2771	.3150	.3072	.1007	.2365	.2314	.5321
China (Peking)	.2860	.2660	.3200	.1280	.2200	.2550	.5250
Tibet	.4200	.2000	.3067	.0733	.1469	.2117	.6414
N. Vietnamese	.4283	.2195	.2983	.0539	.1478	.1954	.6568
OCEANIA (S&C Aust.)							
Aust. Abos.	.3867	.6133	.0000	.0000	.3781	.0000	.6219
Fijians	.4350	.3400	.1650	.0600	.2249	.1194	.6557
New Guinea (natives)	.4189	.3302	.1896	.0613	.2197	.1344	.6459
Marshall Iss.	.5221	.2139	.2109	.0531	.1432	.1415	.7153
Cook Iss.	.4201	.5056	.0520	.0223	.3131	.0379	.6490
Easter Island	.4020	.5986	.0000	.0000	.3660	.0000	.6340
NEW WORLD							
Eskimo (W. Alas.)	.3808	.4408	.1307	.0477	.2854	.0938	.6208
Navaho	.6910	.3060	.0020	.0000	.1670	.0010	.8320
Sioux	.6808	.2885	.0269	.0038	.1588	.0155	.8257
Cherokee	.9559	.0368	.0073	.0000	.0186	.0037	.9777
Maya	.7656	.1667	.0542	.0135	.0944	.0343	.8713
Zapoteco	.8905	.1095	.0000	.0000	.0563	.0000	.9437
Mapuche (Chile)	.7946	.1356	.0698	.0000	.0704	.0355	.8941
Mato Grosso Indians (Brazil)	1.0000	.0000	.0000	.0000	1.0000	.0000	.0000

Mourant, A. E. 1958. THE DISTRIBUTION OF THE HUMAN BLOOD GROUPS. Oxford: Blackwell Scientific Publications.

information directing this development consists of genetic instructions, coded in the deoxyribonucleic acid sequences contained in the chromosomes within the nucleus of the cell. Since these developmental sequences do not take place within a vacuum, but in the multitude of settings to which the individual is exposed from the instant of conception, differences appear, even between individuals of identical genetic constitution, such as identical, or monozygotic, twins. However, so striking are the similarities, of *monozygotic twins* (individuals derived from the splitting of a single zygote at an early stage of development) that their study provides one basis for elucidating the degree to which variation in phenotypic expression is limited by genetic factors.

The major source of genetic information in the study of inheritance in man comes from the collection and analyses of pedigrees, such as the diagrammatic representation of a sample pedigree in Figure 1. The student of human genetics cannot have recourse to controlled breeding experiments on his subjects, but must rely on identifying pedigree patterns from the study of many such pedigrees covering numerous kindreds to determine the precise mode of inheritance for a particular trait. From countless investigations, the mode of inheritance for a large number of known traits has been determined and is consonant with the mechanisms by which the hereditary material contained in the chromosomes is transmitted from parents to offspring.

During *meiosis* (the process of reduction-division in the formation of gametes), each chromosome duplicates itself and, after two sequences of nuclear division, four cells are produced, each containing only one member each of the twenty-three pairs of chromosomes present in the original parent cell. In the male, all four of the *gametes*, or sex cells, thus produced

can become viable spermatozoa, each containing the *haploid* number of chromosomes (N = 23). Only one of the four cells produced during meiosis in the female can become a viable *ovum*, or female gamete, but the ovum produced will also contain the haploid number of chromosomes. When the spermatozoan fertilizes the ovum, the *diploid*, or 2N, chromosome number characteristic of the species (2N = 46 in humans) is reconstituted. Subsequently, through *mitosis*, or somatic cell division, the original cell repeatedly divides and begins to differentiate and develop into an individual human being.

Figure 1. A Sample Pedigree

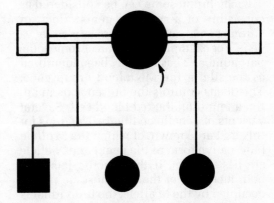

Explanation of symbols:
□ = male
○ = female
parallel horizontal bars = marriage line
vertical lines = descent line
affected individuals shown by black symbols
propositus, or affected individual whose discovery has led to the collection of the pedigree, is indicated by the arrow.

As a consequence of chromosomal segregation and assortment, a parent passes on to his or her offspring a random collection of chromosomes derived from the grandparents of the child. The child may receive twenty-three chromosomes derived from the father's father, or twenty-three chromosomes derived from the father's mother, or any possible combination of chromosomes derived from the father's father and father's mother, while the gamete contributed by the mother will also consist of a random assortment of chromosomes received from her mother and father. Thus, each parent contributes only one member of each chromosome pair to a gamete, while the particular combination of chromosomes contributed varies with each gamete produced. The analysis of pedigrees is based on the recognition of these facts and allows the observer to interpret the pedigree as consistent with the known details of the meiotic process.

Each chromosome can be considered as consisting of a series of genetic *loci,* or chromosomal sites, each occupied by a gene. For example, a locus on chromosome pair number 2 has recently been identified as the site of the MN blood group gene. This locus controls the presence of an antigen found on the red blood cell. Several variants of genetic coding instructions for this trait are known, of which the M *allele* (alternative form of the gene) and N allele are best known. If the specific locus on both members of the chromosome pair is occupied by the M allele, the individual is said to be *homozygous,* and his *genotype,* or genetic constitution, at that locus would be MM, while he would express the M blood type phenotype. If both members of the chromosomal pair carry the N allele, the (homozygous) genotype is NN, while the phenotype is N blood type. However, if the locus on one member of the chromosomal pair is occupied by the N allele and the M allele occupies the corresponding site on the homologous chromosome, the individual is *heterozygous* (MN genotype), and such a person can be phenotypically distinguished from either homozygote.

If two heterozygote (MN) parents produce several children, they might produce children who vary in this respect from one another. Since each parent could produce gametes carrying either the M allele or the N allele, the possible combinations of the different kinds of gametes could lead to the production of children who might carry the MM, MN, or NN genotype. The possible combinations from such a mating can be envisioned in diagrammatic form, as shown below.

Possible zygote combinations from a heterozygote (MN) by heterozygote (MN) mating:

FATHER (MN)
gametes

		M	N
MOTHER (MN) gametes	M	MM	MN
	N	MN	NN

For many traits known in man, the phenotype of the heterozygote cannot be distinguished from the phenotype of one of the homozygotes. For example, in recessive albinism the affected individual is an albino with genotype aa, whose phenotype can be readily distinguished from the phenotypes of individuals with either the AA or Aa genotype since the affected individual shows marked differences in skin, hair, and eye color. However, it is not possible to distinguish the phenotype of the heterozygote from that of the individual carrying the genotype AA. In such cases, the presence of a single allele, sometimes called the *dominant* allele, ensures that the trait is expressed in the phenotype of both the homozygote (AA) and heterozygote (Aa). In contrast, a *recessive* allele is phenotypically expressed only in the homozygous (aa) condition in recessive albinism.

The essential features of the ABO blood

group system can be explained by assuming that any two of three known alleles at this locus can occupy the chromosomal site responsible for the determination of this antigenic grouping. The three alleles—A, B, or O (denoted in some texts as I_A, I_B, or i)—can be present in any combination of allele pairs, but the presence of the A allele or the B allele in combination with the O allele results in the presence of, respectively, the A antigen or the B antigen on the surface of the red blood cell. As a result, either the AA genotype or the AO genotype is expressed in the phenotype as A blood type, while B antigen will be expressed on the red blood cells of a person with either BB or BO genotype. However, when both the A and B alleles are present together in the genotype, the resultant phenotype is AB blood type, while O blood type is expressed only when both alleles at this locus are O, or OO genotype. Thus, the ABO blood group system involves both codominance and dominance-recessiveness in phenotypic expression. Table 2 presents a summary of the salient features of the ABO blood group system described here.

TABLE 2

SIMPLIFIED SUMMARY OF THE GENETICS OF THE ABO BLOOD GROUP SYSTEM

Genotype	Phenotype (Blood Type)
AA(I^AI^A)	A
AO(I^Ai)	
BB(I^BI^B)	B
BO(I^Bi)	
AB(I^AI^B)	AB
OO(ii)	O

In males and females, twenty-two pairs of chromosomes consist of two homologous members of each pair, called *auto-somal chromosomes*. The two members of the twenty-third pair, the X-chromosomes, are similar in females, while a male has a single X-chromosome, along with a Y-chromosome which differs in size and shape from the X-chromosome. These two chromosomes in contrast to the autosomal chromosomes are called the *sex chromosomes* and the presence of the Y-chromosome determines the development of the zygote into a male offspring. The female, whose genotype is, of course, XX, can only produce X-bearing gametes, while the male can form gametes containing either the X- or Y-chromosome. If an X-bearing spermatozoan fertilizes an ovum, the zygote will normally develop into a female, while a male will normally develop from an ovum fertilized by a Y-bearing spermatozoan. Although a number of X-linked genes have been identified, there is only rare evidence that the Y-chromosome contains genes other than those concerned with sex determination. A woman, who has two X-chromosomes, and thus has two alleles at all X-linked loci, may be homozygous or heterozygous for such sex-linked genes. A male, however, having only one X-chromosome, is said to be *hemizygous* at any locus on the single X-chromosome.

The patterns of expression of traits for which the genetic coding information is carried on the X-chromosome differ somewhat from modes of phenotypic expression involving the autosomal chromosomes. Since the male's X-chromosome is received from his mother and transmitted to his daughters, neither the mother nor daughters would necessarily express a trait present in the phenotype of the hemizygous male, depending on the allele present on the other X-chromosome of such females. A female, heterozygous for an X-linked gene, could expect to see the trait expressed in half of her male offspring who, of course, receive only the

Y-chromosome from their father. Some forms of partial colorblindness are controlled by a locus on the X-chromosome. A heterozygote female (who would, herself, not be partially colorblind), married to a male carrying the allele for normal color vision, could produce daughters with normal color vision (with genotype CC or genotype Cc), but her sons could have either normal color vision (C-) or partial colorblindness (c-).

Many other traits in man, such as stature, skin color, and weight, may involve a *polygenic* system of inheritance. Such traits express the effects of a number of loci, and are often referred to as quantitative characters. Since the effects of different alleles at each locus are usually relatively small, identical phenotypes may be the outcome of the action of a number of genotypes, and the phenotypic expression of such characters is frequently subject to considerable modification by environmental factors. It has been estimated, for example, that at least five loci are involved in the inheritance of skin color, but differences in the degree and extent of exposure to sunlight can seriously affect the phenotypic expression of the genetic potential of different individuals. Genetic

analysis of such traits is more difficult than for monogenic traits, and often requires the use of computer facilities, but the principles of inheritance remain unchanged.

While an introduction to the basic principles of genetics may seem to imply an unvarying, one-to-one correspondence between genotype and phenotype, this is rarely the case. Essentially, the genotype codes for a range of phenotypic expression. While that range of expression is relatively limited in some traits, such as the ABO blood group system, much greater variability can be expected in the expression of many other traits. Polydactyly, the presence of supernumerary (extra) fingers and toes, has been studied in many kindreds in which the mode of inheritance has been determined as involving the presence of a single "dominant" allele. The phenotypic expression of this trait in such families varies, however, so that individuals carrying the allele in heterozygous combination may have six or seven fingers on one or both hands, in combination with five, six, or seven toes on one or both feet. Comparisons of monozygotic twins, who are genotypically identical, raised together in a common environment, with identical twins raised apart provide some

TABLE 3

AVERAGE DIFFERENCE BETWEEN THE TWO MEMBERS OF IDENTICAL TWINS,
NONIDENTICAL TWINS, AND PAIRS OF SIBS, REARED TOGETHER;
AND IDENTICAL TWINS, REARED APART.
(from Stern, 1973:661)

Difference In	Identical	Nonidentical	Sibs	Identical (Reared Apart)
Height (cm)	1.7	4.4	4.5	1.8
Weight (kilogram)	1.9	4.5	4.7	4.5
Head length (mm)	2.9	6.2	——	2.20
Head width (mm)	2.8	4.2	——	2.85

Source: Stern, 1973:661

(From PRINCIPLES OF HUMAN GENETICS, Third Edition, by Curt Stern. W. H. Freeman and Company. Copyright © 1973)

idea of the extent of phenotypic plasticity of various traits, while comparisons of data from identical twin pairs with data collected from dizygotic twins or sibling pairs provides one method of estimating the relative influence of genetic and environmental factors influencing the expression of a trait (Table 3).

The chance combination of genetic materials contained in each gamete, and the combination of two such gametes to form a viable zygote, guarantees that virtually no two individuals ever born (except monozygotic twins) have ever had identical genotypes. In addition, genetic variation can be enhanced by *mutation*, which may be inclusively described as changes in the structure, composition, or arrangement of the genetic material. Interactions at the intragenic, genic, cellular, and intrauterine level contribute further to phenotypic variation, while the environmental range to which the individual is exposed after birth ensures that individual variation will characterize the phenotypes of even those individuals who have identical or similar genotypes.

Individual members of a *Mendelian population* (community of interbreeding individuals) are derived from and contribute to a gene pool which is at least partially isolated from other Mendelian populations. Predictably, the frequency of various alleles differs from one such population to another, much in the way that a series of samples from a larger number (or "population") of red and black marbles is likely to differ from each other or from the frequencies of red and black marbles contained in the original group.

When localized breeding populations, or *demes*, are subject to different environmental conditions, these genetic differences may be augmented by the operation of evolutionary forces, so that considerable interpopulation variation results. One plausible explanation of population differences in skin color concerns the production of vitamin D in humans living under very different environmental conditions. Since vitamin D can be manufactured from precursor substances on the skin where ultraviolet rays from the sun are available, lighter-skinned populations are advantaged in northern climates where exposure to the sun is limited by climatic and seasonal factors. A deficiency of vitamin D can lead to rickets, a disease which, if untreated, can be fatal in children and so seriously affect normal bone growth as to impair normal birth delivery in affected women, so that natural selection may well have influenced the present distribution of light-skinned populations. In more equable climatic regimes, and particularly in tropical regions, the filtering effect of darker pigmentation, reducing the amount of ultraviolet radiation exposure, may have proven advantageous since an excess of vitamin D production can lead to calcification of soft tissues.

As a result of genetic and developmental processes, individuals within a population invariably differ phenotypically from one another. Evolutionary processes, including natural selection, operate at the population level to produce polymorphic populations within a polytypic species. Human populations differ not only phenotypically, but each is characterized by a gene pool which is unique to each group. Changes in the gene frequencies of each population through time are a result of evolutionary processes operating on the gene pool of each population under the changing environmental conditions to which it must adapt.

Bibliography

Mourant, A. E. 1958. *The Distribution of the Human Blood Groups*. Oxford: Blackwell Scientific Publications.

Stern, Curt. 1973. *Principles of Human Genetics*. 3rd ed. San Francisco: W. H. Freeman and Company.

For Further Reading

Asimov, I. *The Genetic Code*. Signet Science Library Book. New York: New American Library, 1962. Highly readable, but somewhat outdated, summary of the basic principles of molecular genetics.

Fraser, A. *Heredity, Genes, and Chromosomes*. New York: McGraw-Hill Book Company, 1966. A well-illustrated, clearly written introduction to classical genetics and population genetics of animal populations including extensive materials dealing with humans.

McKusick, V. A. *Mendelian Inheritance in Man*. Catalogs of Autosomal Dominant, Autosomal Recessive and X-linked Phenotypes. 3rd ed. Baltimore: Johns Hopkins Press, 1971. Computerized catalog of genetic traits in Man, arranged by mode of inheritance, and including relevant citations of research reports.

McKusick, V. A. *Human Genetics*. 2nd ed. Englewood Cliffs, N.J.: Prentice-Hall, Inc., 1969. An excellent and lucid introduction to Mendelian genetics and population genetics.

Stern, Curt. *Principles of Human Genetics*. 3rd ed. San Francisco: W. H. Freeman and Company, 1973. Comprehensive and detailed survey of human genetics, including an introduction to probability as applied to genetics problems.

2 | Heredity-Environment Interactions and Population Variation

Animal populations are distributed in space and time and, to survive through time, must obtain the necessities for survival and reproduction of individual members from within the limits of the habitat, or the utilized area as characterized by common vegetational, climatic, topographic, or other significant factors. The means by which a group of related organisms exploits the resources of the habitat and the significant features of the environment which influence the continuing biological success of the population serve to describe the *ecological niche* of each biological population. While the study of the relationships between animals and their environment, or the *ecology* of animal populations, must consider influential features of the physical environment and the biotic environment, the study of human ecology must also consider cultural factors influencing the size and distribution of human populations.

Since it would be impractical in most cases to attempt to identify every feature of the total environment of a population, ecological studies tend to delineate the effective environment, specifying those features of the total environment which serve as limiting factors on the continued survival or growth of the population. *Limiting factors* are those essential elements which singly, or in interaction with other substances, are essential to the organism's survival and reproduction. When these factors are present in such limited amounts or in such abundance as to exceed the tolerance range of the population, inhibition of the survival or growth of the population will occur.

To an ocean dwelling shark, water is unlikely to act as a limiting factor, but the oxygen content of water at various depths would be a predictably significant condition for the survival of this marine organism. The availability of oxygen to terrestrial desert dwellers is much less likely to be a critical variable in explaining population size and distribution than the occurrence and reliability of water sources. A group of related organisms which relies on a particular plant food would be susceptible to the results of any plant disease which attacked the essential food item. Thus, by examining the limiting features of the physical and biotic environment, including behavioral factors and social phenomena, a description of the effective environment can be developed.

Members of a localized human population who share a common core of socially transmitted set of ideas, values, and attitudes, may differ from members of other human populations in their mode and form of utilization of environmental resources. Although a rich and unexploited source of dietary protein exists in the dog population in the United States today, few

11

Americans view "Bowser" as a potential food item and, should the notion be advanced, most respondents would view the suggestion with strong feelings of revulsion. Yet, this is not universally true and dogs are considered an eminently suitable part of the diet in many human societies. Similarly, natives of the northern Gilbert Islands are reported to view the *Portulaca* plant as a relatively innocuous and useless growth, although the residents of the southern Gilbert Islands regularly turn to the hardy plant as a dietary item during periods of drought when more succulent and desirable foods become unavailable.

Man, then, is uniquely subject to the limitations of the *cognized environment*, a restricted range of biotic and physical environmental potential consistent with prevailing ideas, attitudes, and values of the human population utilizing the resources of a region. Shared knowledge and common practices of exploiting the resources of the habitat, as well as the technological means available to a group, serve importantly to define the parameters of the ecological niche of each human population. Thus, the large, artificially irrigated, agricultural enterprises of the "Anglo" populations of southern California and Arizona have virtually supplanted the smaller farms and crops of earlier Indian horticulturalists of the region. On the other hand, a few hundred thousand nomadic, hunting and gathering, Australian aborigines have been reduced in number and relocated in space by European immigrants and their descendants who have applied a highly sophisticated technology to effect a very different level of exploitation of that country's resources.

Among the characteristic features of a biological population is the dynamic attribute of growth. The inherent capacity for population growth is usually referred to as *biotic potential* and refers to the theoretical maximum rate of growth which a popu-lation might achieve if optimal conditions prevailed. If a population occupied an ideal environment, one with abundant resources and lacking competitors and predators, and within which reproductive performance could be maximized, it would be possible to attain the maximum intrinsic rate of increase (r_{max}). This theoretical maximum is rarely realized and usually only for brief periods in the early stages of colonization of an unused habitat or niche by an invading population. Under laboratory conditions, for example, an exponential rate of population growth may be achieved during the early stages of colonization by a few fruit flies established in a jar with large amounts of nutrient media made available.

The maximum fertility potential has not been realized in any human population and would require that women experience a set of circumstances never recorded in any population. These conditions would include, minimally: maintenance of a continuing high level of *fecundity* (biological capacity to reproduce) during the entire reproductive period; entrance into sexual union at an early age; opportunity for sexual unions during all periods when the female was in an ovulating stage; and absence of breast-feeding of children, since this practice tends to suppress or inhibit ovulation. In fact, the highest total fertility of any human population has been recorded among the Hutterites of North America where a rate of 10.4 livebirths has been noted for women of postreproductive age. A comparative study of fertility in various societies reveals that the total fertility of most human populations is far below that of the Hutterites.[1]

Davis and Blake have devised an analytical framework for studying cultural influences on human fertility which recognizes

1. Ludwik Krzywicki, *Primitive Society and its Vital Statistics* (London: Macmillan and Company Ltd., 1934).

three categories of factors—intercourse variables, conception variables, and gestational variables.[2] For example, factors influencing the formation and dissolution of unions during the reproductive period ("intercourse variables") affect the amount of the reproductive period spent after or between unions. Until recent decades, every widow among the Tiwi of north Australia was required to remarry while still at the graveside of her recently deceased husband, thus ensuring that no widow need spend any significant amount of time without the opportunity for intercourse within a sanctioned union. In contrast, the famous Mānava-dharmasastra, or laws of Manu, specified that the remarriage of Brahmin Indian widows was strictly forbidden, so that even the youngest widow must remain celibate throughout the remainder of her lifetime. Differences in contraceptive knowledge, techniques, and practices among human populations provide ready examples of "conception variables" which can affect the fertility levels of human populations, while variation in practices concerning the care and treatment of pregnant women expectably influence the reproductive performance of women in different societies ("gestational variables").

The intrinsic rate of increase (r), as measured by the number of times the population actually multiplies per generation in an unlimited environment, has been studied for four human groups for which adequate documentation is available. During the early settlement period in the history of Tristan da Cunha, Pitcairn Island, Bass Strait islands, and of the Nanja horde of the Australian Maraura tribe, a doubling, or in the case of the Nanja horde, a tripling, of the population took place in every generation over a relatively brief period in the early history of these groups (Figure 2). Over long periods of time, however, birth rates and death rates in a closed

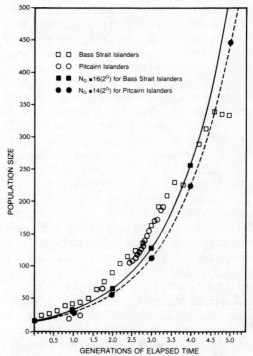

Birdsell, Joseph B. 1957. "Some population problems involving Pleistocene Man," pp. 47-69 in COLD SPRING HARBOR SYMPOSIA ON QUANTITATIVE BIOLOGY, vol. 22.

FIGURE 2. Intrinsic rate of increase for Pitcairn and Bass Strait Islanders.

population tend to attain a state of equilibrium so that there are only minor fluctuations around a relatively stable equilibrium level. The equilibrium point, or the point at which the growth rate stabilizes at zero, is designated as the *carrying capacity of the environment*. The checks on the biotic potential of the population are imposed by *environmental resistance*, the operation of limiting factors which inhibit further continued growth.

Many ecologists have attempted to divide the limiting factors of population growth into those which influence birth

2. K. Davis and J. Blake, "Social structure and fertility: an analytic framework," *Economic Development and Cultural Change* 4(1956):211-235.

and death rates as a function of population density ("density-dependent effects") and those which operate independently of population density ("density-independent factors"). A tidal wave, or tsunami, which inundates an island and drowns 90 percent of the population is an efficient limiting factor which has a density-independent effect. In contrast, very high population densities may provide optimal conditions for increased predation, competition for limited resources, or disease. It is often difficult to categorize single causes of long-term population regulation into this kind of typology since interaction of factors may be involved, and a complex, often polemic, literature has arisen on the subject. In human populations, cultural factors serve as further inhibition to simplistic interpretations.

The rate of growth of a closed population is a result of the balance between births and deaths, and the realized intrinsic rate of increase (r) in a real and imperfect environment is always less than the maximum possible rate of increase. Genotypes with a high intrinsic rate of increase would predictably be at an advantage in populations subject to repeated radical environmental fluctuations or which have just colonized new habitats, while genotypes conferring an enhanced ability to compete under crowded conditions should be more favorable in established populations living in more stable environmental situations. Additionally, the gene pool of populations occupying different habitats and subject to different sets of environmental pressures would expectably differ in the frequency of alleles conferring reproductive success to organisms with different genotypes. A basic principle of population genetics, the Hardy-Weinberg model, provides a means by which the effects of such evolutionary pressures on the gene pools of living populations, can be examined.

Essentially, the Hardy-Weinberg principle provides a rather simple mathematical demonstration that gene frequencies will remain unchanged from one generation to the next *providing* that certain ideal conditions prevail. Suppose that every adult member of a large population was examined for the presence of the antigens of the MN blood group system with the following results:

phenotype
numbers: M = 25,000   MN = 50,000
                   N = 25,000   Total = 100,000

phenotype
frequencies: M = .25   MN = .50
                    N = .25   Total = 1.00

genotype
frequencies: MM = .25   MN = .50
                    NN = .25   Total = 1.00

Since the M allele is present in pairs in the homozygous genotype (2 x 25,000 = 50,000 M alleles) and also, singly, in the heterozygote (M = 50,000 alleles), there are 100,000 M alleles in this population. Similarly, 100,000 N alleles are also present, so that the allele frequencies for this population are M = .50 and N = .50. If mating is at random in respect to this trait and there is equal contribution of each genotype, the frequency of genotypes in the next generation will remain unchanged. This can be visualized in terms of mating crosses, substituting "p" for the value of the frequency of the M allele and "q" for the frequency of the N allele:

$$\text{Males}$$

	$p_M = .50$	$q_N = .50$
$p_M = .50$	$p^2_{MM} = .25$	$pq_{MN} = .25$

Females

$q_N = .50$	$pq_{MN} = .25$	$q^2_{NN} = .25$

or $(p_M + q_N)^2 =$

$$p^2_{MM} .25 + 2pq_{MN} .50 + q^2_{NN} .25 = 1.00$$

Since the model specifies the constancy of allele frequencies and their distribution in genotypes from generation to generation, the formula given above is sometimes used to derive the expected distribution of genotypes in those cases in which the heterozygous phenotype is indistinguishable from the phenotype of one of the homozygotes. For example, a metabolic abnormality involving the absence of an enzyme required to convert phenylaline, an amino acid present in many foods, into tyrosine results in the accumulation of phenylpyruvic acid in the body. The resultant condition, termed PKU-deficiency, is manifested, in part, by impaired mental function, and, through pedigree analysis, has been shown to occur in individuals with a homozygous recessive genotype. In a hypothetical population in which 1 percent of all individuals were affected, the frequency of the allele could be calculated as $q = .10$ (the square root of .01, or q^2). Consequently, the frequency (p) of the allele responsible for the presence of the required enzyme would be .90 (1.00 minus q). Since the frequency of heterozygotes is specified as 2pq by the Hardy-Weinberg formula, the resultant estimate of the frequency of the heterozygote genotype would be 2pq, or .18.

Under the conditions specified by the assumptions of the Hardy-Weinberg principle, the frequencies of genotypes in a population are determined solely by the allele frequencies of the parental population and these frequencies will remain unchanged from one generation to the next. In addition to assumptions related to the size of the population and the opportunity for random mating within the population, panmixia, the Hardy-Weinberg model is further restricted by the assumption that evolutionary mechanisms are not operating to produce changes in the genetic structure of the population over time. Changes in the genes as a result of muta-

tion (see page 9), or the loss of addition of genes as a result of emigration or immigration (gene flow) can result in differences between the allele frequencies of parental and offspring generations. Variation in the sex ratio, in the number of offspring produced by each adult, or in the frequency of matings between genetic relatives can alter the effective size (N_e) of the breeding population, thus providing amenable conditions for the operation of genetic drift, or variance in allele frequencies due to gametic sampling between generations. Natural selection at the genetic level, the differential contribution of specific genotypes to successive gene pools, is probably te most important mechanism influencing the allele frequencies over a number of generations. Thus, the study of living populations is directed to detecting and explaining variations from the conditions and predictions derived from the theoretical model of a hypothetical population.

In fact, many studies fail to detect differences between the observed data and the distribution of genotypes predicted by the Hardy-Weinberg model, even when the structure of the population is demonstrably deviant from that assumed to exist under model conditions. Where significant deviations between observed and predicted results are found it is evident that the population is not in genetic equilibrium (Hardy-Weinberg). However, the Hardy-Weinberg principle does not apply where the assumptions of the model are not met, and where this is the case, the absence of differences between observed and predicted results does not demonstrate that evolutionary mechanisms are inoperative, but only that more sensitive or complex methods of analysis are required to detect their operation. A review of several studies in anthropological genetics may serve here to illustrate how deviations from the predictions or conditions of the Hardy-Weinberg model are used in the analysis of data collected from human populations studied by anthropologists.

A finding of significant differences in allele frequencies between generations or in a population studied at two different time periods clearly violates Hardy-Weinberg predictions of stability in gene frequencies across generations. The results of blood-typing studies among the natives of Saipan Island in Micronesia, carried out by Japanese researchers prior to World War II, stand in contrast to findings recorded in 1964 by Hainline, as shown in Table 4. A comparison of the allele frequencies indicates that the B allele has increased in frequency, while the allele O has decreased significantly between the time of the initial studies and the later period when blood-typing results were collected. Such statistically significant changes might be due to any number of factors, including sampling error in a finite population or nonrandom mating, but the more plausible explanation consistent with ethnographic reports and demographic data traces the changes to the infusion of genes from the large number of Japanese civilians and military troops stationed on Saipan Island prior to 1945 (gene flow). The direction of the changes is consistent with known ABO blood group distributions in Japanese populations which are characteristically high in the frequency of the B blood group. It should

be noted, however, that even where significant differences between observed and predicted results are found, the causes of such changes can only be identified by further analysis.

Although more sophisticated mathematical formulae provide models for considering the influence of evolutionary forces on the genetic constitution of populations, such models remain simplified approaches to more complex realities. No model in population genetics can begin to handle the interactions of biological and cultural factors underlying human diversity. Yet it is precisely in this realm that the anthropologist's unique contribution can be made to an understanding of human variation. The geneticist who studies other animal species is neither concerned with, nor trained to study, the influence of ideational frameworks or "cognitive maps" on the genetic structure of populations. When two populations of Angora rabbits are brought together, matings are not constrained by notions of ethnic identity and exclusiveness. But such ideas often prevail when human populations meet and are apt to restrict random mating. Thus, while a considerable amount of gene flow took place between Japanese troops and the native population of Saipan Island, very few cases of Japanese-native matings have been recorded on the nearby island of Yap where large numbers of

TABLE 4

ABO BLOOD GROUP STUDIES AMONG NATIVES OF SAIPAN ISLAND

	Total Number	Phenotypes (frequencies)				Alleles (frequencies)		
		O	A	B	AB	r_o	p_a	q_b
Pooled results of studies by Takasaki and Misaitsu, cited in Boyd, 1939	678	.522	.288	.128	.062	.723	.177	.084
Data from hospital records examined in 1964	1057	.472	.281	.201	.046	.687	.181	.133

(Reprinted from "Blood typing data, ABO and Rh(D), collected from hospital records in Yap and Saipan: a brief note," HUMAN BIOLOGY, Volume 37, No. 2 (May 1965), by L. J. Hainline, by permission of the Wayne State University Press.)

Japanese personnel were also stationed until the end of World War II. Prevailing attitudes among the Yapese as to the inherent undesirability of such matings seem to have played an important role in maintaining a rigid barrier to interpopulation mating.

The operation of natural selection provides a different context within which biocultural factors can be shown to influence human variation in response to environmental pressures. Natural selection, the process through which a population adapts to its environment, is viewed by most evolutionists as the prime mechanism responsible for the maintenance and patterning of variation in all species of organisms. While selection operates against the phenotype which is relatively less suited to the specific environment, the genotype conferring the advantaged phenotype, as a result, contributes differentially to the gene pool of succeeding generations. The individual with a disadvantaged phenotype in a given environment may die before reproducing or produce relatively fewer offspring than do individuals with different genotypes (and correspondingly different phenotypes). The result is to alter frequencies of alleles in the gene pool of the population from one generation to the next.

Selection may operate against one allele at a locus, most commonly by removing the allele when it is expressed in the phenotype of the recessive homozygote (*homozygote selection*). Infants born with ichthyosis congenita, a condition in which the skin is penetrated by deep bleeding fissures, rarely survive for more than a brief period after birth in any environmental setting. Since the condition is invariably fatal, the allele is removed whenever it appears in the homozygous combination. Presumably, this rare allele is maintained at its very low frequency by recurrent mutation and is transmitted by unaffected parents who are heterozygous at this locus.

Selection may also operate against both alleles at a locus, or in favor of the heterozygous genotype. The result of this *heterozygote advantage* is the maintenance of both alleles in the gene pool at frequencies dependent upon the relative disadvantage of the two homozygotes to each other. This form of selection has been implicated in the maintenance of the sickle trait hemoglobin condition among populations where malaria is constantly present in the region (endemic falciparium malaria).

The major function of hemoglobin, a conjugated protein found in the red blood cells, concerns the transport and transfer of oxygen and cell respiration products in the body. Several deleterious variants of hemoglobin have been identified in human populations at frequencies higher than the levels expected if homozygote selection had been effective. One such variant, sickle hemoglobin, is expressed in the phenotype of the homozygote (Hb^SHb^S) as sickle cell anemia, or sicklemia, a debilitating anemia which, in the absence of medical care, is often fatal before the affected individual reaches adulthood. The sickle cell trait expressed by heterozygotes (Hb^AHb^S) entails a decreased capacity for oxygen transport and transfer, but affected heterozygous individuals do not suffer the severe anemia present in the affected homozygote. Expectably, the fitness (expressed in terms of reproductive effectiveness) of individuals with sickle cell anemia is very low, while individuals with the sickle trait phenotype could be expected to produce relatively fewer offspring than individuals homozygous for the normal hemoglobin allele (Hb^AHb^A).

The presence of the sickle allele in rather high frequencies in parts of Africa was found to coincide generally with the distribution of falciparum malaria. Subsequently, it was suggested that the heterozygote (HbAHbs) was more resistant to infection by the malarial parasite than the HBAHbA homozygote, and when volunteers were infected with the malarial parasite, *Plasmodium falciparum,* heterozygotes showed a significantly higher degree of resistance. Since, on the other hand, the HbsHbs homozygote has a lowered reproductive fitness as a consequence of severe anemia in either the malarial or nonmalarial environment, a plausible explanation of the continued appearance of both disadvantaged homozygotes has been advanced which posits a selective advantage of the heterozygote in an environment in which falciparum malaria

Man, however, had created the environment in which the *Anopholes gambiae* mosquito, which transmits the *Plasmodium falciparum* parasite from person to person, can survive at sufficiently high levels of population densities to maintain endemic malaria in affected populations. As horticulture, or hoe cultivation of plant crops, spread through West Africa, the land clearing activities in which people engaged in the tropical rain forest environment created the stagnant pools which comprise ideal breeding places for *A. gambiae*. And, as these agricultural activities assured greater food supplies, human populations increased in size and adopted more sedentary living patterns than had characterized earlier populations dependent on a hunting and gathering mode of exploiting local resources. In consequence, human groups attained a higher level of population density, ensuring a larger reservoir of infected persons from which mosquitos could continually spread the malarial parasite to others. Thus, the selective advantage of the sickle hemoglobin allele exists in consequence of human activities in exploiting the resources of the tropical rain forest environment!

Our final example represents an attempt to understand the complex interactions of biological, cultural, and environmental factors influencing the genetic composition of a tribal group from South America in which genetic drift could be expected to have been operative. Genetic drift is essentially a nondeterministic phenomenon involving changes in allele frequencies between generations due to gametic sampling, and is a function of the size of the actual breeding population (the number of adults of breeding age). A series of samples of 100 marbles from a jar containing 50 percent red marbles and 50 percent black marbles will not all contain exactly 50 red and 50 black marbles. Rather, it is probable that 95 percent of 100 such samples of 100 marbles will contain either a larger or smaller number of black marbles. Similarly, in a human population of 100, the frequencies of alleles at any locus can be expected to vary somewhat from the frequencies of those alleles in the ancestral gene pool. While formulae have been developed to estimate the expected values of alleles subject to genetic drift, these provide only probability statements about the expected magnitude of change and cannot predict, even in probability terms, the direction of change. A related phenomenon, *founder effect*, concerns variations in allele frequencies of a small population which breaks off from a larger ancestral group. The new founding group represents a small sample of the ancestral population's gene pool and may vary considerably in degree of representativeness of the genetic characteristics of the larger population. As a result of the continued operation of genetic drift, such populations may diverge greatly from each other.

The Yanomamö Indians of southern Venezuela and northern Brazil, numbering between 10,000 and 15,000 persons, are dispersed among some 125 villages in a tropical rain forest environment within which slash and burn techniques of horticulture and limited hunting and gathering of local animals and plants enable the group to support a growing population. The settlement pattern is irregular, but nonrandom, with larger, slightly more populous, villages found at the center of the occupied territory. Internal friction and limited political powers of village headmen militate against the development of villages numbering more than a few hundred residents, while the need for protection from intervillage raiding and hostilities precludes the survival of villages numbering much less than 50 persons, except at the periphery of the tribal area. The resultant settlement pattern is produced by the fissioning of larger villages with dissident factions tending to move toward the distant peripheries of Yąnomamö territory. Chagnon contends that the distances between villages cannot be traced to a shortage of land or competition for resources.[3]

Each village, then, originates when a small founder group splits off from an ancestral village and moves away to form the nucleus of a new village. Predictably, Yąnomamö villages should exhibit a wide degree of genetic divergence by virtue of the sampling variance inherent in the dominant mode of repeated village formation by small colonizing founder groups derived from fissioning of existing villages. In fact, genetic variation among villages does not always fall within the range of expectations provided by models of genetic drift, and a variety of factors are involved. In part, variation in allele frequencies is influenced by the social structure of the Yąnomamö which ensures that the founder groups of new villages include many genetically related persons. This "lineal effect," the result of the formation of a founder group which includes many genetically related persons, tends to enhance genetic microdifferentiation among

Yąnomamö villages. While lineal effect is a random evolutionary force, the fissioning process and the selection process by which the membership of each founder group is determined are engendered by nonrandom, or systematic, cultural prescriptions and social norms.

What can be adduced from the results of the extensive amount of ongoing research into the genetics and ecology of human populations represented by this small, but diverse, sample of such studies? First, it should be evident that human populations are not immune to the environmental pressures which influence the population dynamics of other animal species nor impervious to the operation of those evolutionary mechanisms which affect the genetic constitution of all populations of bisexually reproducing organisms. Despite advanced technologies and the development of synthetic products, the size and distribution of human populations is ultimately dependent on the availability of natural resources as well as the means available for their exploitation and distribution. Rainfall, or, more accurately, the lack of precipitation, has been a limiting factor on populations of the northern parts of sub-Saharan Africa, and thousands have died in recent years as a result of prolonged drought conditions in that region. Natural selection continues to remove, and recurrent mutation to replenish, the allele responsible for congenital ichthyosis in human populations.

Second, it is notable that behavioral patterns play an important role in the operation of evolutionary and ecological processes in many animal species, but the genesis of most behavioral patterns in

3. N. A. Chagnon, "Tribal social organization and genetic microdifferentiation," in *The Structure of Human Populations*, G. A. Harrison and A. J. Boyce, eds. (London: Clarendon Oxford University Press, 1972).

human populations is distinctive, and this fact is of critical significance in the genetic evolution and ecological adaptation of human populations. Reproductive behavior in fruit flies is a relatively direct expression of biological "drives" and results in a high intrinsic rate of increase for any *Drosophila* population in optimal environmental conditions. Reproductive behavior in human populations, however, is never unaffected by the ideational code shared by members of a human society, and the diversity of the complex systems of ideas and values underlying behavioral patterns in different human populations precludes any species-wide characterization of population dynamics. Among the Cheyenne Indians of the North American Plains, voluntary prolonged abstinence on the part of a new father was highly esteemed, and, even if occasionally violated in practice, certainly served to lower the overall fertility rate of Cheyenne wives. In many other societies, a man who has fathered many children is still praised for this evidence of his virility and his demonstrated obedience to the Biblical injunction to "be fruitful and multiply."

Because culture is socially transmitted, largely by means of symbolic communication (human language systems), a range of behavioral plasticity is available to human populations which permits responses to changed conditions more rapidly and effectively than would be possible if such changes were dependent on altered allele frequencies in the gene pool in response to new selective pressures. Fruit flies continue to reproduce until nutrient media are exhausted or metabolic products poison the environment. Human populations can elect to reduce reproductive behavior or to employ contraceptive techniques, to develop or adopt new techniques for exploiting environmental resources without undergoing modifications of anatomical structures or physiological processes.

Heterozygous carriers of deleterious recessive alleles can choose not to have offspring, while females who are heterozygous for deleterious X-linked alleles can use prenatal diagnosis of fetal sex and selective abortion to ensure that they will produce only unaffected female offspring.

Third, it should be obvious that human variation cannot be fully understood simply by reference to the ecological principles or genetic models which suffice in large measure for an understanding of variation in other animal populations. Cultural phenomena constitute an added order of influential variables affecting the maintenance and patterning of variation in human populations and human diversity is the product of complex biological, environmental, *and* cultural interactions. A multitude of forms of interplay and reciprocal feedback relationships between biological and cultural factors influencing the adaptations of human populations to their environments would be required to account for the variation observed in living populations today. However, an appreciation of human variation and of the mechanisms and processes underlying human diversity can be obtained from a more intensive examination of a limited number of forms of biocultural interactions influencing human variation.

For Further Reading

Boughey, A. S. *Ecology of Populations.* New York: Macmillan Company, 1968. A readable introduction to basic concepts and theories of ecology, with strong emphasis on human ecology and evolution.

Johnston, F. E. *Microevolution of Human Populations.* Englewood Cliffs, N.J.: Prentice-Hall, Inc., 1973. Exceptionally clear-cut summary of population genetics applied to studies of human populations, employing a minimum of mathematical expositions.

Mettler, L. E. and T. G. Gregg. *Population Genetics and Evolution.* Englewood Cliffs, N.J.: Prentice-Hall, Inc., 1960. A basic survey of concepts and methods of population genetics applied to studies of variation in animal populations.

Morris, L. N. *Human Populations, Genetic Variation, and Evolution.* San Francisco: Chandler Publishing Company, 1971. A comprehensive review of population genetics, illustrated by selected articles dealing with microevolutionary studies in human populations.

Wilson, E. O. and W. H. Bossert. *A Primer of Population Biology.* Stamford, Conn.: Sinauer Associates, Inc., 1971. A lucid introduction to population ecology and population genetics, with particular emphasis on the use of simple mathematical models.

Bibliography

Birdsell, J. B. 1957. "Some population problems involving Pleistocene Man." *Cold Spring Harbor Symposia on Quantitative Biology* 22:47-69.

Hainline, L. J. 1965. "Blood typing data, ABO and Rh(D), collected from hospital records in Yap and Saipan: a brief note," *Human Biology* 37:174-177.

Livingstone, F. B. 1958. "Anthropological implications of sickle cell gene distribution in West Africa." *American Anthropologist* 60:533-562.

3 | Diet and Human Population Variation

"Man ist was er esst"—"One is what he eats"—is an old German proverb which might well be paraphrased by the ecologist to read "Man eats or he isn't"! Every human population must obtain the nutritional materials required to sustain the metabolic needs of its members from its environment or perish. Yet, populations vary greatly, not only in the nutritional adequacy of the diet available to individuals, but, also, as we have already seen, in the range of potential food sources which are considered appropriate food items.

Standards of nutritional requirements for good health have been established in various parts of the world which purport to establish suggested minimum daily requirements of foods containing "complete proteins," those proteins containing the essential amino acids required for adequate biological functioning, as well as appropriate amounts of carbohydrates, and fats, along with foods supplying necessary amounts of minerals and vitamins.

These ideal standards are not met in many parts of the world, often with a consequently high rate of malnutrition or undernutrition recorded in many populations. In many of the developing countries of the tropical regions of the world, the *synergistic*, or compounding, effect of malnutrition and infection is the primary cause of poor health, especially among children. In more developed countries, overnutrition and obesity, as well as unbalanced nutrition resulting from diets containing, for example, excessive amounts of (expensive) animal fats, have been implicated in increased mortality associated with atherosclerotic conditions and related cardiovascular impairments.

Stini has suggested that man's recent assumption of an agricultural niche has exposed many populations to a form of nutritional stress not experienced by earlier hominids who occupied a hunting-gathering-scavenging niche in which both animal and vegetable foods provided an adequate supply of all necessary amino acids. He argues that the proportional reduction in body size observed in a number of populations relying on agricultural exploitation of only a few vegetable crops represents an adaptive response to resultant nutritional imbalances.[1] This form of adaptation need not entail genetic changes, and the recent, documented increase in average stature of many populations in the United States, Europe, and Japan might reflect attainment of the gene-

1. W. A. Stini, "Evolutionary implications of changing nutritional patterns in human populations," *American Anthropologist* 73 (1971): 1019-1030.

tic potential in populations which have experienced improved dietary conditions in recent generations. A reduction in body size in areas where protein resources are limited would enable more individuals to survive on the limited resources available. A response of this kind to environmental (nutritional) stress would seem an adaptive adjustment of the affected populations. In many cases, less felicitous responses to dietary stress have been made.

Bolton, for example, has described a complex interaction of biological and ecological factors contributing to high levels of aggression among the Qolla Indians of the Andean Highlands through their contributions to the development of *hypoglycemia* (lowered blood sugar levels) in many members of this population. Since brain tissue oxidizes carbohydrates almost exclusively, prolonged hypoglycemia can result in a serious suppression of the oxidative metabolism of the brain and cause permanent cerebral damage or death. Before reaching such critical extremes, however, hypoglycemic patients frequently express symptoms of irritability, excitability, and antisocial behavior. Indeed, descriptions of the personality traits of the Qolla and other Aymara speaking groups of this region have persistently used such terms as "hostile," "intense hate," "malicious," "pugnacious," "cruel," and similar epithets. Bolton, moreover, was able to show a significantly high correlation between individuals ranked high in aggressiveness and those showing moderate levels of hypoglycemia on a standard diagnostic test, the glucose tolerance test. He argues that intensive overutilization of land resources by a growing population, depleted soil conditions, and variable weather conditions have resulted in inadequate food production, with the result that the native diet is deficient, both in quantity (*hypocaloric*) and in amounts of protein, vitamins, and minerals consumed. Since episodic attacks of hypoglycemia may be triggered by hypocaloric meals or high carbohydrate meals, followed by intense physical activities, native dietary practices and behavioral patterns are conducive to the physiological response of hypoglycemia. Bolton further contends that the aggressive behavior which accompanies mild hypoglycemia increases the mortality rate and serves to influence some members of the group to migrate out of this densely populated area.[2] Additionally, suspicion and distrust seem to have precluded communal cooperation in economic activities which could enhance agricultural productivity and alleviate some of the stresses on food resources in the region which now prevail.

Acute dietary inadequacies have also been implicated in the etiology of various forms of abnormal or psychotic behavior found in some populations. Following on earlier studies which suggested that calcium deficiency might be a causative factor in the phenomenon of arctic hysteria termed *pibloqtoq* among the polar Eskimo, Rohrl suggests that nutritional deficiencies may contribute to at least the early stages of "windigo psychosis." A variety of symptomatic expressions of this condition have been reported among the Chippewa, Cree, and related North American Indian tribes, but a majority of recorded cases involve an act of cannibalism. In a number of cases, however, a cannibalistic act was averted, and a "cure" effected, by the consumption of a meal containing large amounts of animal fat. Rohrl argues that the accepted treatment—the ingestion of fat—represents an empirical recognition of the causative role of a dietary deficiency in the development of windigo

2. Ralph Bolton, "Aggression and hypoglycemia among the Qolla: a study in psychobiological anthropology," *Ethnology* 12 (1973): 227-257.

psychosis.[3] Although controlled studies, including dietary research, are needed to substantiate this interpretation, the hypothesis that certain forms of psychopathologic behavior are behavioral responses to dietary inadequacies is consistent with the demonstration of dementia as a characteristic symptom of pellagra, a deficiency disease among impoverished corn eaters, and a growing body of data concerning the biochemical bases of human behavior. The nutritional value of cannibalism may be questionable in terms of energy-expenditure-to-protein-value ratios, as Garn and Block have suggested,[4] as well as being socially disruptive, but, as a source of essential vitamins or fatty acids required for the utilization of some of the B vitamins, the practice may have been essential for the survival of a population for which shortages of such elements acted as limiting factors.

In other populations, genetic adaptation may have played an important role in adjustments to dietary practices. The subject of population differences in nutritional needs as a result of evolutionary adaptations of populations to differing dietary environments, or *genetotrophic adaptation*, has received increased attention in recent decades, and the best known case of this kind concerns lactase deficiency, the absence of an enzyme required to metabolize the carbohydrate lactose present in milk and milk products. While the majority of infants in all human populations produce adequate amounts of lactase during the period of infancy and early childhood, large numbers of adults in many populations are deficient in lactase production and may experience serious symptoms of gastric distress after consuming milk or milk products. Presumably, strong selective pressures have operated in all populations against any allele responsible for infant hypolactasia, and a genetic model has been suggested which specifies

that three alleles may occupy the locus which controls lactase production, L, 1_1, or 1_2. LL homozygotes or the heterozygotes L1_1 or L1_2 would produce lactase throughout the individual's lifetime, but $1_1 1_1$ homozygotes would produce lactase only during infancy and childhood, while $1_2 1_2$ homozygotes would lack lactase as infants. The remaining heterozygote $1_1 1_2$, would presumably produce lactase during infancy, but fail to produce the enzyme during childhood.

McCracken has suggested that adult lactase deficiency represents a survival of the prevailing condition in human populations dating from a distant evolutionary past, and that a selective advantage of the lactase enzyme in adults has existed only with the domestication of animals and the invention of dairying. He has derived support for this hypothesis from a comparison of reported frequencies of lactase deficient adults in populations in which milk consumption is high with those in which there is little or no milk consumption by adults. High to very high frequencies of adult lactase deficiency have been reported among hunters and gatherers, such as Australian aborigines and Greenland Eskimos, while low frequencies for the enzyme deficiency have been recorded from such traditional herding peoples as the Batutsi and Bahima of Africa. Similarly, low frequencies of the enzyme deficiency have been recorded in many populations with high milk production and variable but generally high consumption of milk and milk products by adults (English, Euro-Australians), but higher frequencies are recorded in a number of populations characterized by

3. V. J. Rohrl, "A nutritional factor in Windigo psychosis," *American Anthropologist*, 72 (1970): 97-101.
4. S. M. Garn and W. D. Block, "The limited nutritional value of cannibalism," *American Anthropologist* 72 (1970): 106.

dairying but with no milk consumption by adults (Thais of Southeast Asia, Bantus of Africa). While further research is needed to support the hypothesis presented to explain the observed correlations, McCracken's interpretation is consistent with what is known of the operation of natural selection in human populations and provides suggestive evidence of the operation of biocultural interactions in the development of human population variation.[5]

Another possible example of genetotrophic adaptation concerns the "Chinese restaurant syndrome," a group of variable symptoms expressed by sensitive individuals who consume appropriate amounts of monosodium L-glutamate (MSG), a common food additive frequently used in various parts of the world and in the preparation of certain Chinese dishes. The symptoms are usually merely discomforting in susceptible adult subjects, and may include headache, a burning sensation over parts of the body, and chest pains. However, experimental studies in newborn mice and monkeys reveal that brain damage and lesions can be induced by the administration of large amounts of MSG. Consequently, MSG has been removed from many prepared infant foods in the United States to avoid any possibility of toxic effects on human infants. Although the precise genetic basis of sensitivity to MSG in adults has not been established, differences in reported incidences of the syndrome in various parts of the world suggest that populations differ in the frequencies of sensitive adults and, presumably, in allele frequencies for this trait.

In recent years, considerable research has been devoted to the problem of the influence of malnutrition on the neurological development of the fetal brain with contradictory results. It has been claimed, for example, that lowered average performance levels on intelligence tests by black children in the United States may reflect, in part, impaired development of the brain and nervous system as a result of malnutrition during pregnancy. Extensive studies on various laboratory mammals indicate that severe malnutrition of the mother, especially at certain critical periods in the development of the fetal nervous system, results in impaired learning and behavioral patterns in the offspring after birth. However, while severe food shortages in European countries during World War I and World War II were accompanied by declining birth rates and reductions in average birth weights, no comparable increase in fetal mortality was recorded. Moreover, advances in the study of the metabolic patterns of pregnant women suggest that adaptive alterations are made in the mother's metabolism well in advance of the period when the developing fetus might impose any nutritional stress.

The most comprehensive retrospective study of this question has been based on an analysis of the records of 125,000 males born in Holland between January 1, 1944 and December 31, 1946, who were inducted for military service at about nineteen years of age. Many of these young men were born in Western Holland during the wartime period of severe famine of 1944-45, while others, the "control population," were born in cities of eastern, northern, and southern Holland which had greater access to food supplies during this period. Stein et al. concluded from this study that there were no detectable effects on the mental performance of these young men whose mothers had experienced severe starvation during pregnan-

5. R. D. McCracken, "Lactase deficiency: an example of dietary evolution," *Current Anthropology* 12 (1971): 479-517.

cy.[6] Indeed, a growing body of evidence suggests that the developing human fetus is remarkably well buffered against the effects of nutritional stress, although possibly at the expense of the mother's health.

The newborn infant and the growing child are not protected by the mechanisms which promote physiological homeostasis during gestation. Many studies have attempted to demonstrate the deleterious effects of nutritional stress experienced by malnourished young children. However, nutritional inadequacies are commonly found in association with impoverished social and economic conditions and are often compounded by the effects of infectious diseases and parasitism. Since experimental studies of the effects of malnutrition on growth and development cannot be extended to human populations, a great deal of current research has concentrated on studies of "natural laboratories." The research includes longitudinal and cross-sectional studies of the patterns and rates of child growth and maturation in relatively homogeneous, rural, peasant communities designated as malnourished by any of a variety of criteria.

A series of extended investigations in rural Guatemalan communities exemplifies this approach. These studies consistently reveal a pattern of retarded growth performance in affected village children which begins at about three to six months of age and finally results in the small adult body size characteristic of populations in such areas. For example, Blanco and his associates have illustrated this pattern of retardation in height and weight for 1,412 children from nine Guatemalan rural villages in comparison to standards established by well-nourished children from Central America (Figure 3). Comparable growth patterns in preschool age children have been observed in many parts of the world where protein-calorie malnutrition prevails and are commonly interpreted as

evidence that retarded growth patterns represent a developmental, rather than genetic, adjustment to common environmental conditions by different populations.

Researchers in these areas have consistently stressed the synergistic interaction of malnutrition and disease in affected populations, noting that the nutritional status of the child begins to decline at about the same time that the passive immunity acquired before birth diminishes. The Guatemalan village child who is still being nursed begins to receive contaminated and nutritionally inadequate supplementary foods at about the age of six months, and, by the end of the weaning period, is receiving a hypocaloric, protein-deficient diet while also experiencing a high incidence of diarrheal diseases ("weanling diarrhea"). Moreover, such communicable childhood diseases as measles and whooping cough are most prevalent during the preschool years in these rural communities and are present at a time when the child is already weakened by the combined effects of nutritional inadequacies, parasitism, and repeated bouts of diarrhea. Mata et al. have shown an association between infectious diseases and failure to gain weight in a group of Guatemalan village children studied over a two-year period,[7] while Blanco and others have demonstrated that Guatemalan village children with osteological evidences of previous acute infections or serious physiological stress (Harris lines of the long bones) show a tendency to be

6. Z. Stein, M. Susser, G. Saeger, and F. Marolla, "Nutrition and mental performance," *Science* 178 (1972): 708-713.

7. L. J. Mata, J. J. Urrutia, and B. Garcia, "Effect of infection and diet on child growth experience in a Guatemalan village," in *Nutrition and Infection*, G. E. W. Wolstenholme and M. O'Connor, eds. (Boston: Little, Brown and Company, 1968), pp. 112-126.

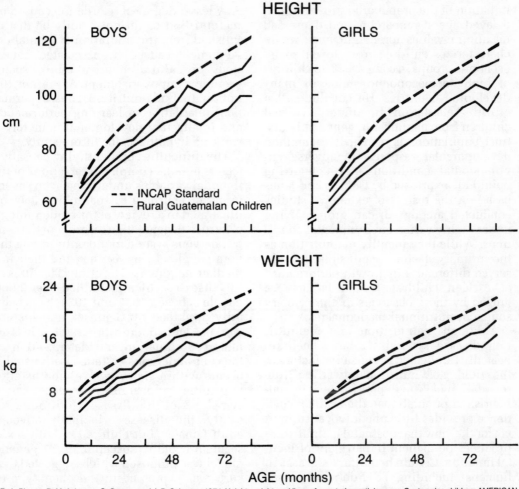

HEIGHT

BOYS

GIRLS

120

100

cm

80

60

- - - INCAP Standard
— Rural Guatemalan Children

WEIGHT

BOYS

GIRLS

24

16

kg

8

0   24   48   72

0   24   48   72

AGE (months)

R. A. Blanco, R. M. Acheson, C. Canosa and J. B. Salomon. 1974. Height, weight, and lines of arrested growth in young Guatemalan children. AMERICAN JOURNAL OF PHYSICAL ANTHROPOLOGY, 40: 39-47.

Figure 3. Mean height and weight ± 1 standard deviation for 1,492 Guatemalan children shown by three continuous lines, compared with standards for Guatemalan children indicated by the discontinuous line, prepared by the Institute of Nutrition of Central America and Panama.

shorter than children lacking such lines.[8]

Another approach to the study of the variables influencing growth and development in children entails comparisons of growth performance and functional maturation in children of different socioeconomic status. Guzman reports that retarded bone development, delayed

8. R. A. Blance, R. M. Acheson, C. Canosa, and J. B. Salomon, "Height, weight, and lines of arrested growth in young Guatemalan children," *American Journal of Physical Anthropology* 40 (1974): 39-47.

initiation of the prepubertal growth spurt, delayed age at menarche, and depressed maximum values for height and weight characterizes children from lower socioeconomic groups in comparison to children of high socioeconomic status in many developing countries. He concludes that growth retardation in underprivileged children from a number of genetically distinct populations is primarily a common developmental response to adverse environmental conditions.[9] A concurring opinion is expressed by Collins and Janes based on the results of extensive studies conducted among African groups living under highly varied environmental conditions. While they identify malnutrition as the primary factor responsible for observed differences in growth performance of African children, social factors are judged by these observers as the primary source of nutritional inadequacies.[10]

Although malnutrition and malnutrition disease synergisms have been repeatedly implicated as causative factors in the etiology of "nutritional dwarfing" (the retardation of growth performance in malnourished populations), the available evidence provides little unequivocal support yet for the view that postnatal malnutrition produces permanent impairment of mental function. Certain hereditary diseases in humans, including PKU-deficiency (see page 15), involve the faulty metabolism of nutrients and are frequently associated with impaired mental functioning, while acute deficiencies of certain vitamins (notably B_6, A, and folic acid) have been implicated in impaired brain development, brain function, and sensory (visual) acuity. However, prolonged, severe starvation sufficient to produce irreversible impairment during the period of maximum neurological sensitivity to nutritional stress in the very young child might well prove so disabling to adequate physiological functioning as to result in early death.

Any lesser degree of retardation caused by malnutrition could not readily be distinguished from the inhibition of mental development caused by associated conditions of cultural deprivation or socioeconomic impoverishment. At present, the notion that malnutrition causes permanent retardation of learning performance and intellectual development is merely a working hypothesis for future study.

The difficulties of identifying causative factors and the complex interactions of influential variables underlying even severe forms of neurological pathology may be illustrated in a review of the epidemiology of *kuru*, a degenerative disorder of the central nervous system found only among the Fore people of New Guinea and their immediate neighbors. The clinical features of this disease, which had killed over 2,000 people between 1957 and 1973, have been fully described by Gajdusek and his coworkers and include progressive loss of motor coordination and deterioration of the central nervous system. Death usually occurs within six to twelve months after the initial appearance of recognizable symptoms of the disease. Until quite recently, the disease principally affected adult females, but children of both sexes seemed equally susceptible. A genetic model was proposed which suggested that kuru was expressed in the phenotype of homozygous or heterozygous children of both sexes and in the homozygous or heterozygous adult female, but occurred only rarely in the heterozygous adult male.

9. M. A. Guzman, "Impaired physical growth and maturation in malnourished populations," in *Malnutrition, Learning, and Behavior*, N. S. Scrimshaw and J. E. Gordon, eds. (Cambridge, Mass.: M.I.T. Press, 1968), pp. 42-54.

10. W.R.F. Collins and M. Janes, "Multifactorial causation of malnutrition and retarded growth and development," in *Malnutrition, Learning, and Behavior*, N.S. Scrimshaw and J. E. Gordon, eds. (Cambridge, Mass.: M.I.T. Press, 1968), pp. 55-71.

Within the last decade, however, the incidence of kuru has declined drastically among the Fore, more noticeably among women than men, and more markedly among children than adults. The implications of these changing patterns led to more intensive investigations which eventually resulted in the identification of a slow-acting virus as the causative agent of the disease and the detection of ritual cannibalism as the means of natural transmission of the virus. Since women and children are the most active participants in such feasts, the gradual disappearance of ritual cannibalism among the Fore since 1957 has reduced their exposure to contamination from the highly infectious brain tissue of deceased kuru victims and altered the patterns of incidence of the disease.[11]

Just as the old "nature vs. nurture" controversy proved to be a spurious and unproductive controversy, rigid and unidirectional cause → effect explanations of human variations in response to nutritional stresses fail to consider the mutually reciprocal influences and additive effects of the interactions of biological, cultural, and physical influences affecting adjustments of human populations in differing historical and environmental settings. A constant theme of many nutritional studies in human populations has been the assumption that metabolic patterns and needs are universal and that, while a limited range of individual variability is recognized, no significant population differences exist. Various health organizations have acknowledged the desirability of adapting recommended nutritional standards to be expressed in terms of specific food resources available in local areas, but little concern has been given to the possibility that populations may differ in nutritional requirements, in the ability to metabolize recommended foods, or in the practical advisability of introducing new food items into established dietary patterns.

A classical example of this biased view has been demonstrated by the disastrous results which often followed the distribution of powdered milk supplies by governmental and welfare agencies attempting to improve the nutritional status of children in developing countries. The drastic increase in incidence of gastrointestinal disorders and diarrheal diseases which followed the introduction of powdered milk in many of these communities can be related to the prevalence of lactase deficiency in some of these populations. In part, too, the results can be ascribed to the consequences of preparing packaged foods for consumption under poor hygienic conditions or where suitable, safe water supplies are scarce or lacking.

The substitution of commercially prepared foodstuffs has usually been associated with a shift from a subsistence economy to participation in a cash economy, usually with deleterious effects. (In technologically advanced societies, many foods must be artificially enriched to replace important elements removed by commercial techniques of preparation, and educational campaigns are conducted to encourage consumers to utilize less extensively altered ingredients.) In the expanding port towns and mining centers of some Melanesian islands, bottle-feeding of infants has been widely adopted. The adoption of this practice provides one means by which migrants from more traditional communities express their altered social status and acceptance of "modern" ways. However, since wages are not always reliable or adequate for the demands

---

11. D. C. Gajdusek and C. J. Gibbs, Jr., "Subacute and chronic diseases caused by atypical infections with unconventional viruses in aberrant hosts," in *Persistent Virus Infections*, Perspectives in Virology, 8 (New York: Academic Press, Inc., 1973), chap. 15.

of town living, the nutritional status of the child may actually suffer and the rate of disease increase as an open can of milk must be repeatedly diluted with contaminated water to conserve cash outlays until the child is receiving grossly hypocaloric feedings. The substitution of bottle-feeding for breast-feeding at a very early age has resulted in a decrease in the average age at which diarrheal diseases are most common, and the infant mortality rate has actually increased in a number of developing countries in recent years as child mortality rates have decreased. It should not be overlooked, either, that suppression of lactation removes a physiological constraint on ovulation so that bottle-feeding may also contribute to increasing birth rates!

Dietary practices and patterns constitute a domain of human behavior in which cultural-environmental interactions impinge forcefully on the biology of a population and its individual members. As we have seen, cultural factors influence not only *how* environmental resources are exploited and modified for consumption, but also *what* potential biotic resources are actually utilized. The biological (and demographic) attributes of a population also affect the adequacy and effectiveness of prevailing modes of utilizing environmental resources. Population pressure in areas of limited resources can evoke disruptive social responses and deterioration of living standards as well as the aggressive personal behavior expressed by Qolla victims of hypoglycemia. Infants receiving a nutritionally adequate diet, but suffering from endemic gastrointestinal infections, regularly succumb to the resultant conditions of dehydration and electrolyte imbalance.

Prevailing dietary practices and patterns specify the limits within which the individual members of a population must seek to satisfy the nutritional requirements essential to life. Since populations differ in respect to dietary history and environment, corresponding differences in such characteristics as body size, developmental patterns, or the presence or absence of specific digestive enzymes, are both expectable and welldocumented. It has been generally assumed that nutritional dwarfing represents a common developmental response to nutritional adequacies present in diverse diets of impoverished populations throughout the world. This results in a reduction of interpopulation variation, but in an increase in intrapopulation variation among groups in which marked socioeconomic differentials exist. However, a developmental vs. genetic explanation may be a specious argument since it seems likely that natural selection has operated on the gene pools of populations subject to chronic undernourishment in favor of genotypes underlying such phenotypic plasticity, e.g., by removal of children lacking the ability to respond to nutritional stress through a reduction of metabolically demanding growth needs. There is now some evidence that genetic differences for specific enzymes (e.g., lactase) may characterize populations with different dietary environments, while recent studies in New Guinea suggest that human variation may also be expressed in the form of differing physiological responses and efficiencies in food metabolism.

In brief, dietary practices and patterns seem to have played a large role in the maintenance and patterning of human variation as different dietary environments have led to varied forms of genetic, developmental, physiological, and, perhaps, behavioral responses by human populations.

For Further Reading

Berg, A. *The Nutrition Factor.* Washington, D.C.: The Brookings Institution, 1973. Report of the nutritional consequences of industrialization in developing countries, with particular emphasis on the results of breastfeeding practices.

Jeliffe, D. B. *Infant Nutrition in the Subtropics and Tropics.* 2d ed. Geneva: World Health Organization, 1968. Survey of the status of nutritional conditions and associated medical problems in children of developing countries.

Roe, D. A. *A Plague of Corn.* The Social History of Pellagra. Ithaca: Cornell University Press, 1973. An eminently readable account of the history of the identification of the nutritional deficiency underlying pellagra.

Scrimshaw, N. S. and Gordon, J. E., eds. *Malnutrition, Learning, and Behavior.* Cambridge, Mass.: M.I.T. Press, 1968. A series of collected articles dealing with results of studies in animal and human populations by outstanding authorities in these fields.

Bibliography

Behar, M. 1968. "Prevalence of malnutrition among preschool children of developing countries." In *Malnutrition, Learning and Behavior,* Edited by N. S. Scrimshaw and J. E. Gordon, Cambridge, Mass.: M.I.T. Press, pp. 30-41.

Norgan, N. G.; Ferro-Luzzi, A.; and Durnin, J. V. G. A. 1972. "An investigation of a nutritional enigma." *Human Biology in Oceania* 1:318-319.

4 | Demography and Human Variation

It is possible to compare populations in terms of size (number), density, persistence, ecological efficiency, or other measures of biological success, but any exercise of this kind is of little value to our understanding of human variation without an appreciation of the demographic processes responsible for observed differences and similarities. Two populations may be identical in size and density, yet these similarities may be maintained by very different values and relationships between the *vital rates* (birth, death, marriage, and migration rates) characterizing each group. A *stationary population,* a stable population which is not changing in size, may be the consequence of high mortality (death) rates in combination with high fertility (birth) rates or result from the balance between low fertility and low mortality rates. The age structure of two such populations would be drastically different, as could be seen by comparing the characteristic *population pyramid* (a diagrammatic representation of the age and sex composition of a population at a given time) of both groups. A population pyramid (Figure 4) represents the outcome of vital rates operating in previous years, and a broad base often designates a growing population, while a narrow base may represent the results of low fertility or high infant and child mortality.

A more comprehensive expression of the interrelationships between birth and death rates and the age structure of a population is found in the *life table,* a table indicating the number of survivors from a *birth cohort* (the number of individuals born during a given period of time) to each successive age, based on a specific set of death rates for each age category, or *age-specific death rates* (Table 5). A basic model in the scientific study of populations is derived from Lotka's classic demonstration that if constant age-specific birth and death rates prevail, a population will gradually achieve a stable age distribution, with subsequent growth or decrease in size occurring at a constant rate. A great deal of demographic research has been devoted to evaluating the effects of changing age-specific birth and death rates on the age-sex structure of populations and, as in the application of models in population genetics, more sophisticated formulae have been developed for these purposes.

Unfortunately, the more elegant techniques of demographic analysis have seldom been utilized in anthropological research, in part because of the absence or incompleteness of certain kinds of population data and reliable vital statistics for most native groups. Since many of the populations studied by anthropologists are of limited size, a rare epidemic or an unusually large number of births during a single year may indicate a spuriously high crude birth or death rate. Howell has questioned if lack of adequate long-term data or faulty data may not account in large measure for some of the seemingly extreme deviations in vital rates and demographic structure of native populations studied by anthropologists compared to the documented range of variation in such attributes established from studies in larger populations for which extensive census materials and vital records exist.[1] However, radical fluctuations in population size or vital rates would have great evolutionary significance, and any "averaging" of deviations to fit theoretical expectations based on populations with different histories and characteristics obscures a major potential source of human variation.

One of the most striking phenomena of this century has been the rapid population growth of many nations, particularly in Latin America, Africa, Asia, and parts of Oceania. Demographers have developed projections of future population growth trends which forecast a depressing picture of an overcrowded, starving world population if demographic trends in the indus-

1. N. Howell, "The feasibility of demographic studies in 'anthropological' populations," in *Methods and Theories of Anthropological Genetics*, M. H. Crawford and P. L. Workman, eds. (Albuquerque: University of New Mexico Press, 1973), pp. 249-262.

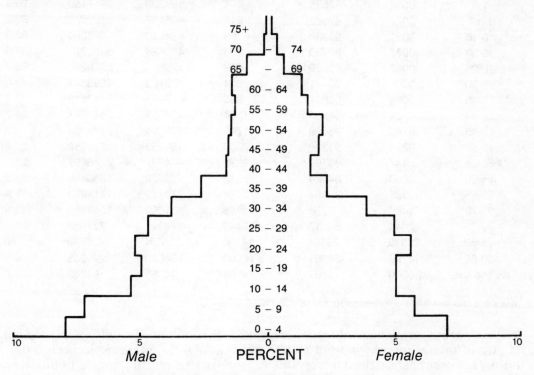

Figure 4. Population Pyramid, Chamorros of Guam, 1897
(N = 8,698)

TABLE 5

ABRIDGED LIFE TABLE FOR THE
TOTAL POPULATION OF THE UNITED STATES, 1964

Age Interval	Proportion of 100,000 born			Stationary population		Average Remaining Lifetime
	Dying	Alive				
Period of life between two exact ages stated in years (1)	Proportion of persons alive at beginning of age interval dying during interval (2)	Number living at beginning of age interval (3)	Number dying during age interval (4)	In the age interval (5)	In this and all subsequent age intervals (6)	Average number of years of life remaining at beginning of age interval (7)
x to x + n	n_{q_x}	1_x	n_{d_x}	n_{L_x}	T_x	e_x
0-1	.0247	100,000	2474	97811	7015291	70.2
1-5	.0038	97526	374	389209	6917480	70.9
5-10	.0022	97152	216	485177	6528271	67.2
10-15	.0021	96936	203	484222	6043094	62.3
15-20	.0047	96733	453	482626	5558872	57.5
20-25	.0063	96280	609	479905	5076246	52.7
25-30	.0066	95671	634	476793	4596341	48.0
30-35	.0085	95037	807	473261	4119548	43.3
35-40	.0120	94230	1134	468503	3646287	38.7
40-45	.0183	93096	1700	461534	3177784	34.1
45-50	.0284	91396	2600	450953	2716250	29.7
50-55	.0447	88796	3972	434637	2265297	25.5
55-60	.0669	84824	5672	410722	1830660	21.6
60-65	.0985	79152	7794	377213	1419938	17.9
65-70	.1464	71358	10448	331660	1042725	14.6
70-75	.2044	60910	12449	274326	711065	11.7
75-80	.2910	48461	14100	207654	436739	9.0
80-85	.4220	34361	14500	134820	229085	6.7
85 and over	1.0000	19861	19861	94265	94265	4.7

Bogue, D. J. 1969. PRINCIPLES OF DEMOGRAPHY. New York: John Wiley and Sons, Inc.

trializing countries of the world continue at present rates. However, most of man's history has been characterized by very different patterns of population dynamics and the recent history of population trends in Europe and North America offers some hope that continued rapid growth need not characterize the future of our species. Most reconstructions of human population growth suggest that the population of the world increased only very slowly from the time when the first hominids appeared, some few million years ago, until the beginning of the Neolithic period in the Old World, perhaps 10,000 years ago. By 1650, the world's population growth began, with the highest rates of growth observed in industrialized regions of Europe and North America until about 1920 when developing nations of other parts of the world began to grow at a more rapid rate than industrialized nations. Analysis of these patterns reveals that nations differ in characteristic levels of birth rates which are now higher in developing countries than in the highly industrialized countries of the West. What, then, have been the demographic factors responsible for the almost imperceptibly slow rate of population growth during 99 percent of the period when hominids occupied this planet?

In a series of essays which first appeared in 1799, Thomas Malthus, an English clergyman, enunciated a "principle of population" which postulated that unlimited population growth is restricted only by positive checks of famine, war, disease, or other causes of premature death, or by such preventive constraints as postponement of marriage. The biological determinism of this "dismal theory" was challenged by Carr-Saunders who argued that a variety of cultural factors, including voluntary abstinence, infanticide, and abortion are used in varying degrees and combinations in different societies to maintain population size at an optimum level below that at which more severe positive checks would begin to operate.[2] Subsequently, Kryzwicki's ambitious compilation of the vital statistics of many native populations provided a body of comparative data which supported many of Carr-Saunder's arguments.[3]

Tribal societies which are presumably more representative of early human groups than the populations of modern nations, are characterized by a high percentage of children despite the low number of children born and reared per woman. Even if a fairly large percentage of children die before reaching maturity, the long-term result of unrestricted fertility would be a growing population. However, despite early age at marriage and a high nuptiality (marriage) rate, Kryzwicki concluded that the highest average number of children produced by Australian aborigine women was about five, and a variety of practices, including infanticide, prolonged nursing, abortion, and sexual abstinence, were employed which effectively limited population growth. Birdsell has reported that infanticide involved between 15 and 50 percent of all births in certain Australian groups and, as the practice was differentially directed toward females, resulted in an unbalanced sex ratio among adults.[4] This method of family spacing sharply limited the number (and variance in number) of surviving offspring, so that 185 of 194 recorded sibships included between one and five children surviving to adulthood, while only 9 sibships included a greater or lesser number of children who reached reproductive age. Nag investigated the association between fertility levels in sixty nonindustrial societies and a variety of factors, including age at marriage, postpartum abstinence, polygyny, separation or divorce, postwidowhood celibacy, sterility, venereal diseases, contraception, and abortion.[5] A statistically

2. A. M. Carr-Saunders, *The Population Problem* (Oxford: Clarendon Press, 1922).

3. L. Krzywicki, *Primitive Society and its Vital Statistics* (London: Macmillan and Company, Ltd., 1934).

4. J. B. Birdsell, "Some predictions for the Pleistocene based on equilibrium systems among recent hunter-gatherers," in *Man, the Hunter*, R. B. Lee and I. DeVore, eds. (Chicago: Aldine Publishing Company, 1968), pp. 229-240.

5. M. Nag, "Factors Affecting human fertility in non-industrial societies: a cross-cultural study," no. 66 (New Haven: Yale University Publications in Anthropology, 1962).

significant relationship was found only for associations of fertility levels with post-partum abstinence, sterility, and venereal disease in the populations he examined. Indeed, the crude birth rate in many developing nations, for which figures are generally available only during this century, indicates that fertility levels have increased drastically only since 1946, a trend which Bogue ascribes largely to improved health conditions.[6] On the island of Yap, a radical increase in the mean number of live births has been associated with the introduction of antibiotics in 1946, reducing the frequency of urogenital infections and venereal diseases prevalent in that population, and a similar explanation has been offered to account for the recent increase in population growth on Ulithi Atoll. Predictably, relaxation of cultural proscriptions surrounding sexual behavior and improved medical care may facilitate higher levels of fertility in developing countries.

Estimates of mortality in native populations are greatly handicapped by the disturbing effects of contact with alien peoples and the abandonment of traditional customs. Vallois concluded from his survey of ancient skeletal remains that duration of life was shorter and child and female mortality higher in these groups than in skeletal populations of more recent times. While only the rare individual lived past the age of fifty, the presence of even a few aged individuals in the collected remains of very ancient groups suggests that general conditions were not so severe as more sensational reconstructions of man's "brutish, bestial past" might indicate.[7] Interestingly, Lee has reported that the proportion of aged adults (46 of a total population of 466) among the !Kung Bushmen, a modern group of hunters and gatherers living in the Kalahari Desert, compares favorably with the percentage of elderly in many industrialized countries. Moreover,

the evidence of healed fractures in the limb bones of ancient skeletal remains suggests a low incidence of bacterial infections, while the low population densities of ancient hunting-gathering groups would not have been amenable to the maintenance and spread of certain communicable diseases which have influenced the mortality patterns of modern populations.[8]

Dunn has argued that parasitic and infectious diseases, as well as various forms of "social mortality," have contributed substantially to mortality patterns among hunting and gathering peoples.[9] Since parasitic and infectious diseases are closely related to ecosystem diversity, no simple generalization can be applied to all populations of hunters and gatherers. However, some forms of social mortality—cannibalism, infanticide, sacrifice, geronticide, warfare—were probably more frequent in the past than homicide, suicide, or stress diseases.

Native populations in many parts of the world have experienced radical shifts in mortality rates and growth patterns as a consequence of foreign contact and colonization. The persistent decline in numbers reported for many Pacific island populations has attracted considerable attention since the arrival of the earliest Western observers, and many theories have been proposed to account for this widely reported phenomenon in Oceania.

6. D. J. Bogue, Principles of Demography, (New York: John C. Wiley and Sons, Inc., 1969) p. 72.

7. H. V. Vallois, "The social life of early man: the evidence of skeletons," in *Social Life of Early Man*, S. L. Washburn, ed. (Chicago: Aldine Publishing Company, 1961), pp. 214-235.

8. R. B. Lee, "What hunters do for a living, or how to make out on scarce resources," in *Man, the Hunter*, R. B. Lee and I. DeVore, eds. (Chicago: Aldine Publishing Company, 1968), pp. 30-48.

9. F. L. Dunn, "Epidemiological factors: health and disease in hunter-gatherers," in *Man, the Hunter*, R. B. Lee and I. DeVore, eds. (Chicago: Aldine Publishing Company, 1968), pp. 221-228.

For example, the population of Guam, which may have numbered between 30,000 and 50,000 natives when discovered by Magellan, declined to less than 2,000 natives by the beginning of the eighteenth century. Similarly precipitous population declines accompanied the Euro-American colonization of the Marquesan and Hawaiian islands, while less drastic but impressive declines in numbers were recorded for many more island societies.

Psychological malaise, disease, forced emigration, and a host of other explanations have been proposed to account for the decline in population size which characterized most of the Pacific region, but McArthur contends that the demographic consequences of differential mortality from disease epidemics has been a major cause of prolonged depopulation in this area.[10] As a result of differentially high mortality among adults aged 15 to 44 years during the 1918 influenza pandemic in the Fiji Islands, the birth rate for the following years was sharply reduced. Relatively fewer adults of reproductive ages survived the epidemic and many marriages were disrupted by the death of one spouse with the result that a lesser number of births occurred in the years immediately following the epidemic than were reported for previous years. Since the history of many Pacific islands is characterized by the repeated appearance of disastrous epidemics of introduced diseases, the demographic structure of most islands must have been repeatedly disturbed, compounding the direct effects of increased mortality rates.

Wrigley has argued that gross fluctuations in harvest yield, as well as the appalling effects of epidemic diseases, contributed importantly to the population growth history of preindustrial Europe.[11] Students of the historical demography of Europe have shown that the price of wheat provided a remarkably accurate demographic barometer in certain regions: during periods of high prices, the number of burials increased, while the numbers of births and marriages decreased. Following a period of crisis, the number of marriages and conceptions tended to increase greatly, while mortality fell well below the figures recorded during previous critical episodes. In Colyton, a parish of southeast Devon, England, a surprisingly high age at marriage for females (27-30 years) prevailed until the early nineteenth century, and probably played an important role in the low rate of population growth characteristic of the region during this time. During the nineteenth century, lower age at marriage, high fertility rates, and declining child mortality produced increased rates of natural increase in most of Europe, but, by the latter part of the century, marital fertility began to decline to levels lower than ever experienced at any prior time. This change, associated with the spread of the use of contraception to limit family size, has continued as a long-term trend in modern patterns of population growth in most industrialized nations.

In recent decades, many industrializing nations have succeeded in reducing mortality rates, but fertility rates have tended to remain very high or to show only slight reductions. Highly industrialized nations, on the other hand, are characterized by low birth rates and low death rates. A broad appreciation of the genetic and evolutionary significance of different fertility and mortality rates is provided by the results of measuring selection intensities in a number of populations which differ in these demographic characteristics. Crow's index of selection (I) includes one compo-

10. N. McArthur, *Island Populations of the Pacific* (Canberra: Australian National University Press, 1968) pp. 345-354.

11. E. A. Wrigley, *Population and History* (New York: World University Library, 1969) pp. 61-76.

nent of natural selection due to differential fertility (I_f) and another component related to differential mortality (I_m) and has been calculated for a number of populations (Table 6). The results of many such calculations suggest that although differential fertility may be of greater importance in highly industrialized nations today, differential mortality has been the major selective agent throughout human history.

Morgan has calculated the index of total selection intensity for female cohorts of the Ramah Navajo to show the altered relationships between fertility and mortality components of selection potential in this population throughout the course of its history (Table 7). Between 1869 and 1890,

the Ramah Navajo band, joined by a few early migrants, and numbering a total of perhaps 100 individuals, settled in northwest New Mexico. Between 1890 and 1920, a few in-migrating males and children joined the group. In subsequent periods of Ramah Navajo history, increasing migration brought in and removed entire families as well as young adults, until the population numbered about 1,400 in 1971. High fertility of females of the founder period (x) has not been matched by younger cohorts, but intermediate levels of mortality among reproductive females (p_d) until about 1944 has continued to contribute importantly to continuing selection intensities. As mortality trends change,

TABLE 6

SELECTION INTENSITY IN SELECTED POPULATIONS SHOWING MAXIMUM AND MINIMUM I_m AND I_f

Tribal populations	I_m	I_f	I_f/P_s	I_t
1. Bosogo Bantu*	1.778	0.141	0.392	2.170
2. Yao, Nagasaland	0.190	0.349	0.415	0.605
3. Ramah Navaho	0.374	1.572	2.159	2.533
4. Yakö	0.377	0.211	0.290	0.667
State Populations				
1. Bengali Villages	0.456	0.217	0.316	0.772
2. Trinidad and Tabago	0.127	0.875	0.987	1.114
3. Malta and Gozo	0.202	1.028	1.236	1.438
4. Hutterites	0.218	0.136	0.166	0.384
National Populations				
1 & 4. Mexico**	0.490	0.613	0.915	1.405
2. England and Wales	0.036	1.210	1.254	1.290
3. Switzerland	0.062	1.496	1.588	1.650

*The populations are listed in the following order: (1) Maximum I_m, (2) Minimum I_m, (3) Maximum I_f, and (4) Minimum I_f.
**Mexico has both the maximum I_m and the minimum I_f.
Source: Modified from Spuhler, 1962.

Spuhler, J. N. 1960. SEMINAR ON THE USE OF VITAL AND HEALTH STATISTICS FOR GENETIC AND RATIATION STUDIES. New York: United Nations.

the fertility component should assume a greater role in the potential for evolution among the group.

Modification of demographic structure is a response to environmental stress which, in turn, alters the operation of evolutionary forces on populations in all parts of the world. Indeed, the biological fitness of a population, or of a specific kind of genotype within a population, can be specified by the intrinsic rate of increase which is calculated from the age-specific birth and death rates characteristic of the population (Table 8). Accordingly, despite the paucity and incompleteness of extensive population data from many societies, increasing attention has been directed to the influence of demographic factors in the maintenance and patterning of human variation.

Roberts has utilized the intrinsic rate of increase (r) to measure the genetic fitness

of the colonizing population of Tristan da Cunha, an isolated island situated in the south Atlantic Ocean about midway between the Cape of Good Hope and Cape Horn.[12] Although the island was discovered in 1506 and visited sporadically thereafter, attempts to settle the island remained unsuccessful until 1817 when three members of a British garrison posted to the island in 1816 asked permission to remain on the island when the garrison withdrew. The three, along with the Cape-colored wife and children of one of the men, stayed and settled. In the ensuing years, two of the original settlers left the island, while several castaways, deserters, and survivors of shipwrecks joined the colony. In 1827, five Cape women were

12. D. F. Roberts, "Genetic fitness in a colonizing human population," *Human Biology* 40 (1968): 494-507.

TABLE 7

INDEX OF SELECTION CALCULATED FOR THE RAMAH NAVAJO, BASED ON LIVEBIRTH FERTILITY OF FEMALES BORN IN 1844-1924, AS OF 31 DECEMBER 1964.

Interval of birth years of females	$\bar{x}$	$\bar{x}_s$	P_d	P_s	I_m	I_f	I_f/P_s	$I= I_m + I_f/P_s$
1844-89	6.543	6.841	0.111	0.889	0.125	0.289	0.325	0.450
1890-1909	4.174	4.971	0.169	0.831	0.203	0.643	0.774	0.977
1910-24	4.234	5.529	0.268	0.732	0.366	0.518	0.707	1.073
1844-1924	4.660	5.629	0.214	0.786	0.271	0.499	0.634	0.905

Explanation of terms:
I (Index of total selection intensity) = $I_m + I_f/P_s$
I_m (mortality component of index of total selection) = P_d/P_s
I_f (fertility component of index of total selection) = V_f/x_s
V_f = variance in number of births to women of reproductive ages
x = mean number of births to women surviving to reproductive ages
P_d = proportion of liveborn females dying before reproductive ages
P_s = estimated proportion of women surviving to reproductive age

K. Morgan, 1973. "Historical demography of a Navajo community," pp. 263-314 in METHODS AND THEORIES OF ANTHROPOLOGICAL GENETICS, M. H. Crawford and P. L. Workman, eds. Albuquerque: University of New Mexico Press.

imported as wives of male residents, and the total population of the island then numbered seven men, six women, and eleven children.

Analysis of the intrinsic rate of increase of the population, calculated from fertility and mortality histories of cohorts born from before 1815 until 1920 are shown in Table 9. The fertility of the females of the founder group was exceptionally high and has not been matched by any younger cohort, while periods of low or negative rates of increase have been associated with episodes of massive emigration from the island. The genetic effects of repeated population size fluctuations have also been described by Roberts and the consequences of migration of some individuals, along with the resultant differential con-

tribution of nonmigrants to the gene pool, are shown in Figure 5. Obviously, reductions in population size drastically alter the genetic constitution of human populations and constitute a major source of human polytypism.

As Hulse has pointed out, gross differences exist in the relative proportions and genetic characteristics of human populations in consequence of different demographic histories.[13] Thus, the present numbers and distributions of different races must be vastly different from the conditions of earlier periods in human history. For example, the descendants of a few

13. F. S. Hulse, "Some factors influencing the relative proportions of human racial stocks," *Cold Spring Harbor Symposia in Quantitative Biology* 22 (1957): 33-46.

TABLE 8

CALCULATION OF THE EFFECT OF DUODENAL ULCER ON THE FITNESS OF A HUMAN POPULATION
(Based on Italian Census and Life Table Data for Females, 1953)

Age Group	l_x	b_x	k_x	q_x	$q'_x = k_x q_x$ $\times 10^{-6}$	$\delta_x = \sum_{t=1}^{} q't$ $\times 10^{-6}$	$l_x b_x \delta_x$ $\times 10^{-6}$
15-19	0.937	0.0172	0.0023	0.00285	5.795	5.80	0.94
20-24	0.934	0.192	0.00265	0.00395	8.15	13.95	0.28
25-29	0.930	0.34	0.00196	0.00520	10.2	24.15	7.64
30-34	0.925	0.3792	0.00236	0.00655	15.5	39.65	13.91
35-39	0.918	0.1465	0.00225	0.00900	20.0	59.65	0.08
40-44	0.909	0.0867	0.00338	0.01180	39.7	99.45	7.84
45-49	0.896	0.0122	0.0044	0.01770	77.7	177.15	1.94
							40.57

Note: 1_x and q_x come from a standard Italian life table: l_x refers to survival to the midpoint of the relevant age group and q_x is the probability of death in the five-year interval following this mid-point. b_x is the Italian age-specific female birth rate for 1953, given in five-year intervals, calculated as

$$\frac{\frac{1}{2}(\text{number of births to people of age x in a given year})}{\text{total number of people of age x}}$$

kx is the ratio of the number of deaths from duodenal ulcer among females of age x to the total number of deaths among these females. $q'x = k_x o_x$ is the probability of dying from duodenal ulcer in the relevant time interval. The other quantities are calculated as indicated:

$$R_0^0 - Ro = \sum_{t=1}^{n} l_x b_x \delta_x = 40.6 \times 10^{-6}.$$

(From THE GENETICS OF HUMAN POPULATIONS by L. L. Cavalli-Sforza and W. F. Bodmer. W. H. Freeman and Company. Copyright © 1971.)

hundred thousand early immigrants from north and west Europe still exceed in number the millions of migrants from southern Europe who came to the United States at a much later date, while both groups vastly outnumber the offspring of the few hundred thousand Indians who inhabited North America at an even earlier time. Predictably, the relative proportions and distributions of human races will not remain unchanged in the face of differential demographic patterns prevailing now and in the near future.

The forms of biocultural interactions underlying the diverse demographic histories of human populations are often exceedingly complex and varied. Even among natural populations immediately dependent on hunting and gathering of local biotic resources with a relatively limited technology and lacking extensive methods of food preservation, biocultural differences produce sharply distinctive demographic responses to environmental stresses.

Although the dialectical tribes in Australia vary in numbers and composition, the mean value of native tribal populations in this region approximates 500 individuals. For 123 tribes inhabiting inland regions whose water resources depend primarily on rainfall falling within tribal boundaries, a coefficient of correlation of .81 is found between mean annual rainfall and the area occupied by a tribe. In a number of other tribes, deviations from the predicted associations of area and population have been traced to the consequences of diffusion of circumcision and subincision rites. The adoption of these genital mutilations into male initiation rites results in tribal fragmentation by separating the formerly homogeneous dialectical community into "haves" and "have-nots," and by intensifying social relationships between those bands adopting the new practices and the groups from whom such

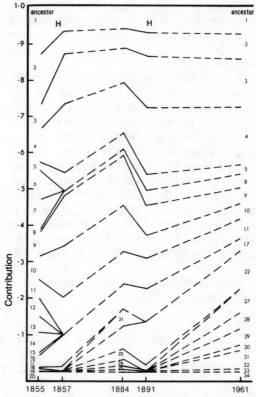

Roberts, D. F. 1968b. "Genetic effects of population size reduction," NATURE, 220: 1084-1088.

Figure 5. Overall contributions of ancestors to the gene pool of the population in 1855, 1857, 1884, and 1961. H shows serious bottleneck.

rites are borrowed. Clearly, among the relatively unclothed aborigines, such symbols of participation are readily observed and serve to distinguish adherents of new patterns of behavior from nonmembers far more readily than the different forms of beliefs and practices distinguish members of different religious groups in this country! In the course of time, reintegration of such fragmented tribes takes place and the equilibrium level of population size and density is restored, but this example sug-

41

gests the extent to which even ritual practices can influence the population history and demographic structure of human populations existing at an economically simple level.

In the stressful Arctic environment, gross differences in the nature of the ecosystem and the mode of its exploitation produced radical differences between the population structures of the Aleuts and of the Eskimo. The residents of the Aleutian Islands were distributed in a linear fashion down the Aleutian Islands chain, and were divided into three dispersed dialectical breeding groups. While only vigorous adult males might hunt such important sea animals as the otter, which constituted perhaps one-third of the native diet, the remainder of the diet was supplied by women and children who collected such other important food items as sea urchins and land plants, and by elderly males who fished in local streams and tidal areas. The large, deployed Aleut population, composed of small units, diverse in age and sex composition, comprised a highly effective mode of organization for utilizing the biotic resources of the Arctic coastal environment. In the more diverse ecological settings occupied by the Eskimo, different patterns of exploitation of land and sea mammals by adult male hunters resulted in very different population structures. Laughlin argues that the excellent nutritional base of the Aleuts was reflected in the attainment of noteworthy longevity, enhancing the complexity and transmission of intellectual and material culture. As anatomy and health practices could be passed on by older persons with considerable experience, improved conditions of health and lowered mortality resulted as

TABLE 9

THE INTRINSIC RATE OF NATURAL INCREASE IN THE TRISTAN POPULATION

Cohort	Women	Men
x -1814	.076	.044
1815-1829	.045	.021
1830-1839	.013	.023
1840-1859	—.006	—.007
1860-1869	.011	.003
1870-1879	—.004	—.002
1880-1889	.010	—.017
1890-1899	.022	.031
1900-1909	.026	.016
1910-1919	.019	.015
Sub Totals:		
x -1839	.036	.032
1840-1879	—.005	—.001
1880-1919	.019	.014
Total:		
x -1920	.016	.013

(Reprinted from "Genetic fitness in a colonizing human population," HUMAN BIOLOGY, Vol. 40, No. 4 (1968), by D. F. Roberts, by permission of the Wayne State University Press)

practitioners of such skills acquired knowledge and training from elderly "cultural librarians."[14]

In many cases, more complex modes of demographic regulation than the direct operation of Malthusian constraints have characterized the population history of human societies. Netting, noting that warfare in technologically simple societies rarely results in large population losses or the acquisition of property or territory, has detected an important, but indirect, demographic consequence of armed conflict among the Kofyar people of northern Nigeria. Although records of armed conflict reveal that loss of life was minimal and fairly evenly divided between opposing sides, such behavior signals to participants a state of disequilibrium between resources and population, while also aggravating the situation as both sides despoiled disputed property, abandoned villages and moved whole settlements into safer, more distant, villages. However, periods of endemic fighting were also accompanied by increased death rates due to disease. Netting argues that the reduction in clearing activities and the regrowth of abandoned villages and land plots which followed armed conflicts provided the opportunity for population increase and spread of the tsetse fly which carries *Trypanosoma gambiense*, the blood parasite causing sleeping sickness (trypanosomiasis) in humans.[15] The tsetse fly, now increased in numbers and distribution, found denser settlements of humans upon which to concentrate. Since this endemic disease (as well as cerebrospinal meningitis, which appears to be associated with overcrowding) has a high fatality rate, the indirect consequences of warfare serve to maintain Kofyar population densities at a level below that at which severe strains on local resources would appear.

Since evolutionary forces operate through demographic mechanisms, the significance of demographic processes in the creation and maintenance of human variation cannot be overemphasized, and, indeed, has been formally recognized as a specific concern in "genetical demography." It seems clear that changing demographic trends characterize the recent history of most human populations so that selection intensities are becoming more directly associated with fertility differentials in populations of industrialized nations, while most of human evolutionary history reflects the operation of the mortality component of selection. This fact does not imply any necessary decrease in human diversity as populations around the world become increasingly integrated into a global industrial economy. The various forms of biocultural interactions underlying even similar forms of demographic response to a universal technology preclude genetic identity in the foreseeable future. The extent of variation already present in the species is so vast that thousands of generations would be required merely to express this potential in all possible genotypic combinations. Nor will the spread of reliable contraceptive techniques and their broad acceptance reduce variation, for, as Dobzhansky has pointed out, the index of selection is even "...greater in populations with small average numbers of children per couple than in those with many children."[16]

Just as mortality differentials have pro-

14. W. S. Laughlin, "Ecology and population structure in the Arctic," in *The Structure of Human Populations*, G. A. Harrison and A. J. Boyce, eds. (Oxford: Clarendon Press, 1972), pp. 379-392.

15. R. C. Netting, "Fighting, forest, and the fly: some demographic regulators among the Kofyar," *Journal of Anthropological Research* 29 (1973): 164-179.

16. T. Dobzhansky, "Natural selection in mankind," in *The Structure of Human Populations*, G. A. Harrison and A. J. Boyce, eds. (Oxford: Clarendon Press, 1972), pp. 213-233.

duced the variation now existing in human populations, fertility differentials will doubtless continue to maintain human variation, although the patterning of future diversity will alter as fertility differentials assume a greater role in the direction of natural selection.

For Further Reading

Barclay, G. W. *Techniques of Population Analysis.* New York: John Wiley & Sons, Inc., 1958. A basic and highly intelligible manual for the mathematical analyses of population data of varied quality and coverage.

Kammeyer, K-C. W. *An Introduction to Population.* San Francisco: Chandler Publishing Co., 1971. A succinct and straightforward introduction to basic demographic concepts and principles.

McArthur, N. *Introducing Population Statistics.* Melbourne: Oxford University Press, 1961. A practical guide for the basic treatment and interpretation of population data, based on the author's extensive work with census materials for Pacific island populations.

Pirie, P. "The effects of treponematosis and gonorrhea on the populations of the Pacific islands." *Human Biology in Oceania* 1: (1972) 8 187-206. Summary account of the devastating effects of one class of diseases on the population history of Oceania.

Polgar, S., ed. *Culture and Population: a Collection of Current Studies.* Monograph 9, Carolina Population Center, University of North Carolina at Chapel Hill. Cambridge, Mass.: Schenkman Publishing Co., 1971. Collection of articles reporting research involving demographic studies in a variety of human populations.

Bibliography

Birdsell, J. B. 1973. "A basic demographic unit." *Current Anthropology* 14:337-356.

Cavalli-Sforza, L. L. and Bodmer, W. F. 1971. *The Genetics of Human Populations.* San Francisco: W. H. Freeman and Company.

Lessa, W. and Myers, G. 1962. "Population dynamics of an atoll community." *Population Studies* 15:244-257.

Morgan, K. 1973. "Historical demography of a Navajo community." In *Methods and Theories of Anthropological Genetics.* Edited by M. H. Crawford and P. L. Workman, pp. 263-314. Albuquerque: University of New Mexico Press.

Morris, L. N. 1971. *Human Populations, Genetic Variation, and Evolution.* San Francisco: Chandler Publishing Company.

Roberts, D. F. 1968. "Genetic effects of population size reduction." *Nature,* 220:1084-1088.

Underwood, J. H. 1973a. "The demography of a myth: abortion in Yap." *Human Biology in Oceania* 2:115-117.

————. 1973b. "Population history of Guam: context of microevolution." *Micronesica* 9:11-44.

5 | Nonrandom Mating and Cultural Selection

Unlike some other less discriminating organisms, humans do not mate at random with their neighbors, but in a highly selective fashion. All societies prohibit marriage or sexual relationships with certain categories of "relatives," but the range of proscribed mates may include not only genetically related persons (*consanguineous relatives*), but also persons who may bear no genetic relationship to each other, such as relatives by marriage (*affines*). In the United States, a bewildering array of state laws variably prohibits marriage between certain consanguineal relatives, related either in a direct line of descent (*lineal relatives*) or collaterally (*collateral relatives*), or between affinal relatives (Table 10). In all states except Georgia, a man is prohibited from marrying such lineal relatives as his mother, daughter, grandmother, or granddaughter. All states ban marriage between such collateral relatives as siblings, but only one state (Oklahoma) bans marriage between second cousins, who are also collaterally related. A large number of states prohibit marriage to certain affines, including son's wife (or daughter's husband), but only two states prohibit marriage to wife's stepdaughter or husband's stepson.

Many societies also specify certain categories of consanguineal relatives as preferred mates. Among the ruling families of ancient Hawaii, Egypt, and Peru, marriage between siblings kept sacred power (and worldly possessions) confined to the royal line. More commonly, a prescriptive principle is applied to indicate whom any member of a society ought to marry. Many societies in Asia, Africa, and Melanesia espouse *cross-cousin marriage,* or marriage with either mother's brother's daughter or father's sister's daughter. Among the Miwok Indians of California, a man was expected to marry his mother's brother's daughter, while among the Trobriand Island natives, the preferred form of marriage took place between a man and his father's sister's daughter. Marriage between offspring of like sex siblings *(parallel cousin marriage)* is a less widespread practice, but is commonly found in a number of Middle Eastern societies. Among the Bedouin, a young man had prior claim to his father's brother's daughter, and payment had to be made to recompense the young man should the girl's father make other arrangements for his daughter's marriage. More distant collateral relatives are also specified as preferred marital partners in a number of societies. Thus, among the Arunta tribe of Australia, a man was expected to marry his mother's mother's brother's daughter's daughter. Affines are also designated as preferred mates in some groups so that marriage of a widow to her deceased husband's brother (*levirate*) is described in the Old Testament, while a number of societies practice the *sororate,* in which a man marries his wife's sister(s) either while his first wife is still living or after her death.

As these examples suggest, all societies prohibit marriage between "kinsmen" as variously defined to include certain persons related by marriage as well as specific consanguineous relatives. Marriage between persons belonging to this prohibited category of kin is termed *incest,* and the prohibition is usually extended to preclude sexual relations as well as marriage between such individuals. Many societies also utilize a prescriptive principle to designate certain categories of persons as preferred mates between whom marriage is not only permissible, but desirable, and this prescription is also often extended to designate acceptable sexual partners as well as spouses. Marital customs requiring marriage within certain specified groupings, as between residents of a village, members of a caste, or citizens of a country, are often referred to as principles of *endogamy. Exogamy,* on the other hand, refers to traditions concerning marriage outside of one's village class, caste, or other social unit. Obviously, these terms may apply simultaneously (e.g., where one must marry outside of his own village, but within his own country) and must be specified in terms of the particular groups

TABLE 10

LAWS AFFECTING MARITAL PARTNER CHOICE IN THE UNITED STATES
(after Farrow and Juberg, 1969)

A man (woman) may not marry his (her)

	Sister (Brother)	Half sister (Half brother)	Niece (Nephew)	Half niece (Half nephew)	Aunt (Uncle)	Half aunt (Half uncle)	1st Cousin	1½ Cousin	Half 1st Cousin	2nd Cousin
Coefficient of inbreeding	1/4	1/8	1/8	1/16	1/8	1/16	1/16	1/32	1/32	1/64
Ga	X	X	X*		X*					
DC, Fla, Me, Md, RI, SC, Vt, VI†	X		X*		X*					
Calif, Colo, Hawaii, Mass, NM, NY, Va	X	X	X		X					
Del, Mich, NH	X		X		X		X			
Pa	X	X	X‡		X		X			
Ala	X	X	X	X	X					
Ariz, Ark, Idaho, Ill, Iowa, Kan, La, Miss, Mo, Mont, Neb, W VA, Wyo	X	X	X		X		X			
Alaska, Conn, NJ, PR, Tenn, Tex	X	X	X	X	X	X				
SD	X	X	X		X		X		X	
Okla	X	X	X		X		X			X
NC	X	X	X	X	X	X	X§			
Nev	X	X	X	X	X	X	X	X		
ND, Ore, Utah	X	X	X	X	X	X	X		X	
Ind, Ky, Minn, Ohio, Wash, Wis	X	X	X	X	X	X	XII	X	X	
Total	53	42	53*	18	53	17	30§II	7	10	1

*Only aunt-nephew marriage prohibited (Ga) (Jews in RI).
†VI indicates Virgin Islands.
‡Implied by aunt and uncle prohibitions.
§Double first cousins only (NC).
IIPermitted when woman is over 55 yr (Wis).

TABLE 10-continued

State or Territory

A man (woman) may not marry his (her)	Conn, Okla, SD	Ala, Miss, Pa, Tex	Tenn	Iowa NH	Ga	Va, W Va	DC, Me, Md, Mass, Mich, PR, RI, SC, Vt, VI*	Total
Father's wife (mother's husband)	X	X†	X	X†	X	X	X	23
Grandfather's wife (grandmother's husband)							X	10
Wife's mother (husband's father)				X	X		X	13
Wife's grandmother (husband's grandfather)							X	10
Wife's daughter (husband's son)	X	X	X	X	X	X	X	23
Wife's granddaughter (husband's grandson)		X	X		X	X	X	18
Wife's stepdaughter (husband's stepson)						X		2
Son's wife (daughter's husband)		X†	X	X‡	X	X‡	X	20
Grandson's wife (granddaughter's husband)			X	X§			X	13
Nephew's wife (niece's husband)						X‖		2

*VI indicates Virgin Islands
†Father's widow specified (Iowa, NH, Tex).
‡Son's widow specified (Ala, Iowa, NH, Tex, Va).
§Grandson's widow specified.
‖Niece's husband only (Va).

A person must not marry

State or territory	Any ascendant or descendant	Any relative within and including the following degree
Alaska		3rd
Ariz	X	
Calif	X	
Colo	X	
Conn		3rd
Del	X	
Fla	X	
Hawaii	X	
Idaho	X	
Ind		5th
Ky		5th
La	X	
Md	X†	
Minn		5th
Mo	X·	
Mont	X	

A person must not marry

State or territory	Any ascendant or descendant	Any relative within and including the following degree
Nev		5th
NJ	X	
NM	X	
NY	X	
NC		3rd
ND	X	
Ohio		5th
Okla	X	
Ore		4th
SD	X	
Tenn	X*	
Utah	X	4th
Wash		5th
Wis		5th
PR	X‡	3rd
Virgin Islands		3rd
Total states and territories	20	14

*Or any ascendant or descendant of either parent.
†Within and including three degrees.
‡Or any ascendant or descendant by affinity.

(Reprinted by permission from the JOURNAL OF THE AMERICAN MEDICAL ASSOCIATION, Volume 209, No. 4 (1969) 534-538.)

within each society to which they refer. However, the term *inbreeding* as used here refers exclusively to matings between consanguineous relatives and is independent of the classificatory systems of kinship relationships found in different societies. Marriage between genetically related persons is also referred to as *genotypic assortative mating* and constitutes one major form of nonrandom mating in human populations.

However emphatic the underlying prescriptions, these preferred marriages between consanguines constitute only a minority of the total number of marriages in any society. Computer simulations as well as ethnographic observations, reveal the effect of demographic constraints influencing the availability of preferred mates of the appropriate age, sex, and genetic relationship in preventing the actualization of such marital preferences in all but a limited number of cases. Thus, societies differ not only in the extent to which inbreeding is encouraged, but also in the degree to which inbreeding actually takes place.

Since the genotypes of genetically related individuals are more likely to be similar by virtue of descent from a common ancestor than the genotypes of two unrelated individuals, genotypic assortative mating alters the distribution of alleles among genotypes to increase homozygosity within the population. Obviously, if the effective population size is small, some degree of inbreeding will inevitably occur since some marriages between genetically related persons are certain to take place. However, this *population inbreeding* has rarely been so influential in affecting genetic homozygosity within human populations as *pedigree inbreeding*, the preferential mating of genetic relatives in accordance with the different marital patterns found among human societies.

At least some studies in population isolates descended from a small founding group have detected unusually high frequencies of pathological genetic conditions which appear only rarely in other groups. Among the Old Order Amish, a religious group living in Pennsylvania, Ohio, and Indiana, four recessive genetic disorders are found at relatively high frequencies. One of these conditions, Ellis-van Creveld syndrome, is an extremely rare disorder, with less than fifty cases reported in the existing medical literature until forty-three definite cases were identified among the Amish population. Similarly, unusually high frequencies of rare genetic disorders or distinctive allele frequencies for more ordinary traits have been reported from other religious isolates, including the Hutterites and Dunkers, and from other genetic isolates such as the Brandywine triracial isolate in Maryland or the population of Tristan da Cunha Island.

The *coefficient of inbreeding* (F) is a measure of the probability that two alleles at a locus are identical by descent from a common ancestor, and can be calculated to estimate the probable degree of homozygosity due to inbreeding for an individual or to provide a mean value for the population. A value of $F = 0$ indicates a complete absence of inbreeding while $F = 1.0$ would indicate complete inbreeding, or self-fertilization. For example, the coefficient of inbreeding for the offspring of a mating between father and daughter is 0.2500; for the child born to a marriage between first cousins 0.0625; and for the offspring of a marriage between third cousins 0.0039. With $F = 0.2500$, there is a 25 percent chance that alleles at any particular locus are derived from the same ancestor, or, conversely, a 75 percent chance (1 - F) that the alleles at that locus are not identical by descent.

Occasionally, outstanding geniuses have appeared from inbred family lines, but

TABLE 11
INBREEDING EFFECTS IN MAN

(Source, Lerner: 1968)

Hiroshima study (from J. V. Neel)

Trait		Noninbred Control	Offspring of First-cousin Marriage	Percent Change
One or more major	Males	7.4	9.0	21.6
defects, percent	Females	9.0	10.3	14.5
Height at 10 years,	Male	130	129	0.4
in cm.	Females	130	129	0.4
Verbal ability	Male	59	55	4.7
test score	Females	57	53	4.8
Average grade in	Male	3.2	3.0	4.0
mathematics	Females	3.2	3.0	4.1

Japan (from W. J. Schull)

Frequency per 10,000 births

Abnormality	First-cousin mating	Second-cousin mating	Unrelated
Club foot	10.5	8.6	9.2
Harelip	17.6	17.2	18.8
All anomalies	84.3	77.5	46.7

J. V. Neel Compilation

Death to various pre-reproductive ages

	Offspring of first-cousin marriages	Offspring of unrelated controls
Negroes		
Brazil	46.0	31.2
Tanganyika	32.1	34.3
Asians		
Japan	13.0	9.1
Europeans		
U.S.A.	16.8	11.6
France	12.2	5.4
Sweden	25.6	31.4
Brazil	31.1	31.1
Germany	32.2	29.5

(From HEREDITY, EVOLUTION, AND SOCIETY by I. Michael Lerner. W. H. Freeman and Company. Copyright © 1968. And with permission from J. V. Neel and W. J. Schull.)

the bulk of medical literature and the results of extensive animal-breeding studies have stressed the deleterious consequences of prolonged, intensive inbreeding (inbreeding degeneration). While human populations have never matched the high levels of inbreeding achieved in experimental studies carried out by plant and animal breeders, studies in a variety of human populations have found evidence that inbreeding effects in man are often detrimental (Table 11).

Since many, perhaps the majority of, deleterious genetic traits are expressed only in the phenotype of the recessive homozygote, the increase in homozygosity caused by inbreeding provides additional opportunity for the operation of natural selection. Thus, in the case of *ichythosis congenita*, described earlier on page 17, the responsible allele is transmitted by heterozygotic carriers. Any increase in the frequency of the homozygous genotype would allow the allele to be removed from the population at a higher rate of elimination than would be possible if mating was entirely random. Consequently, the immediate effect of inbreeding is merely to alter the distribution of alleles into genotypes, but this provides different conditions for the operation of genetic selection.

Other forms of nonrandom mating include positive assortative mating *(homogamy)* between persons similar in respect to certain traits, or negative assortative mating *(heterogamy)* between persons dissimilar in particular attributes. These terms have been applied to mating preferences based on such broadly defined characteristics as social class membership, racial identification, or professional association, or restricted to such character specific features as hair color, height, and weight. In the United States, racial and religious endogamy are more common than class endogamy, while in India, at least until very recently, caste endogamy has been a predominant form of assortative mating. Insofar as a genetic basis for character-specific traits exists, phenotypic assortative matings for such attributes can be related to the genetic basis of human variation. Assortative mating for simple genetic traits can be mathematically demonstrated to alter the distribution of alleles to produce increased homozygosity in the case of positive phenotypic assortative mating, or increased heterozygosity where matings take place between persons with dissimilar phenotypes.

Studies in the United States and Britain have revealed that significant correlations between mates occur in respect to a number of traits, including some for which a partial genetic basis has been established (Table 12). Negative assortative mating for stature has been recorded in a North American Indian population and has been suggested for matings of red haired individuals in Europe and the United States and for albinos in the San Blas tribe of Central American Indians. Although, predictably, phenotypic assortative mating would increase the homozygosity of alleles for traits with simple modes of inheritance, matings between individuals similar in respect to such polygenic traits as stature need have no such consequences since similar phenotypes may result from different genotypes. Different patterns of assortative mating within a population subdivided into smaller isolates may, however, enhance the variability of the larger reproductive community.

Selective mating represents another form of nonrandom mating which has probably played an important role in the evolution of the human species. Darwin, who drew attention to the phenomenon of "sexual selection," described it in terms of a struggle between members of one sex for the possession of members of the other sex, but subsequent investigations have indicated that selective mating practices often involve more subtle and indirect forms of behavior than implied by the term "struggle." Certainly, every human society expresses values and attitudes about what is deemed most desirable in a mate, although these judgments vary greatly from one group to another. Ideals as to the beauty, wealth, power, courage, or other attributes of a suitor may not prevent anyone from marrying eventually, but as these standards may lead to earlier age at marriage, more frequent opportunities for sexual relationships, or a greater number of sexual partners, may affect the differential contributions of more favored individuals to the gene pool of succeeding generations.

TABLE 12

ASSORTATIVE MATING IN HUMAN POPULATIONS IN EUROPE AND THE UNITED STATES

(Source: Lerner, 1968)

Trait	Correlation between Mates
Age	0.76
Memory	0.57
Intelligence	0.47
Ear-lobe length	0.40
Ear-length	0.40
Waist circumference	0.38
Neurotic tendency	0.30
Stature	0.28
Eye color	0.26
Hip circumference	0.22
Weight	0.21
Neck circumference	0.20

(From HEREDITY, EVOLUTION, AND SOCIETY by I. Michael Lerner, W. H. Freeman and Company. Copyright © 1968.)

Hulse has suggested that selective mating of upper-class males to females with fairer skin color has altered the distribution of alleles affecting skin pigmentation among the Japanese. He argues that individual preferences expressing an esthetic preference for lighter skin color have influenced marital choices, even where arranged marriages are common. Since males of good social position are in a better position than their less advantaged peers to seek mates meeting esthetic, as well as practical, standards of esteemed qualities, a differential distribution of alleles for lighter skin color by social class has taken place.[1] In a somewhat parallel process, preferential mating between lighter-skinned segregants descended from matings between American blacks and Euro-Americans in the United States may have accelerated the flow of alleles for lighter skin color out of the American black population in the recent past.

A more common form of selective mating concerns differential access of males to available females. Among the Xavante tribe of Brazil, village chiefs and clan heads are far more likely to engage in *polygynous unions* (simultaneous marriages by a male to two or more wives) than other males in the population, and these village leaders produce two to three times more children than do other males. *"Chief effect,"* the socially conferred reproductive advantage of headmanship, has also been described for the Yąnomamö where, in one case, two headmen sired, between them, some twenty-eight offspring, or one-quarter of the entire village population. In Australia, a complex of demographic restraints and social obligations ensure that old men do get all the girls, many in polygynous unions, despite a highly skewed sex ratio among adults.

However, lest those of us who will not attain high political or social position despair, the race for mates may not always go to the advantaged, but merely to those who

1. F. S. Hulse, "Selection for skin color among the Japanese," *American Journal of Physical Anthropology* 27 (1967): 143-155.

manage to find the right occasion and the appropriate time. Among the Hopi Indians of northeastern Arizona, albinos appear with exceptionally high frequency, particularly among the more highly inbred populations of Second and Third Mesa. The frequency of the allele for recessive albinism (a) is so high that albinos would appear only slightly less often even if random mating prevailed, since over 12 percent of the population are heterozygotes, or unaffected carriers of the allele. The maintenance of the allele in such high frequencies, if not the origin of the trait among the Hopi, has been related by Woolf and Dukepoo to the differential reproductive advantage of Hopi albino males.[2] Since such men do not engage in the farming activities characteristic of males in this society, they have differential access to women who remain in the village while their husbands are working in the corn fields. That such opportunities are not passed by is suggested by Hopi lore which includes statements concerning the sexual accomplishments of these stay-at-home albino males!

Nonrandom mating is scarcely confined to human populations, and, indeed, sexual selection has played an important role in the evolution of striking visual and auditory features used in courtship displays by males in a number of other social species. It also appears that mother-son matings do not take place in natural populations of some nonhominid Primate groups, including among man's closest relatives, the chimpanzees, and this has led some students of animal behavior to speak of "incest tabus" in these groups. Some investigators have also begun to consider the possible reproductive advantage accruing to less aggressive males in some species who survive to propagate by avoiding interindividual conflicts with other males during at least the early stages of mating and establishing of nesting territories. But

in no other species than man does a body of shared ideas, values, and attitudes regulate and specify mating behavior, nor is such ordering so pervasive and disseminated as in human populations.

Propinquity, or geographical proximity, restricts mating behavior in all populations of bisexually reproducing organisms, but human mobility has ensured, to an increasing degree in modern times, that genetic interchange between populations can take place. Culture, expressed in the availability of technological means to remain warm in arctic climates, to prepare toxic foods for safe consumption, to alleviate the disabilities of the sick and infirm, or in any of a host of extrasomatic means of adjusting to environmental stresses, has prevented the evolution of a number of genetically distinct species of hominids. As a result, intermixture can and does take place between members of different human populations whenever the opportunity arises.

On the other hand, man does erect cultural, or artificial, barriers to genetic exchange and create socially approved channels for exchange of mates between social units. The resultant regulation of sexual behavior and marriage patterns is not inflexible, but provides a means for rapid adjustment to changing conditions. It would be naive to think that all barriers to marriage will fall in an enlightened, modern world where rapid means of transportation lead to heightened rates of individual mobility. The barriers of the future will continue to be based on cultural norms, and to affect the genetic composition of human populations, but the geographic boundaries which have partially separated man from his potential mates may be of lesser importance to future

2. C. M. Woolf and F. Dukepoo, "Hopi Indians, inbreeding, and albinism," *Science* 164 (1969): 30-37.

evolutionary trends. Should we already recognize the international "jet set" of modern life as a new form of nonlocalized breeding population?

For Further Reading

Campbell, B. *Sexual Selection and the Descent of Man, 1871-1971.* Chicago: Aldine-Atherton, 1972. Excellent, provocative discussions of the role of sexual selection in human evolution.

Freire-Maia, N. and Freire-Maia, A. "The structure of consanguineous marriages and its genetic implications." *Annals of Human Genetics* (London), 25(1961):29-39. A study of the frequencies and genetic consequences of the various subtypes of consanguineous marriages, particularly among Brazilian populations.

Reid, R. M. "Inbreeding in human populations." In *Methods and Theories of Anthropological Genetics.* Edited by M. H. Crawford and P. L. Workman, pp. 83-116. Albuquerque: University of Mexico Press, 1973. Comprehensive summary covering consanguineous marriage and inbreeding in human populations and the mathematical models used in analyses of inbreeding effects.

Bibliography

Birdsell, J. B. 1972. "Human Evolution." *An Introduction to the New Physical Anthropology.* Chicago: Rand McNally and Company.

Farrow, M. G. and Juberg, R. C. 1969. "Genetics and laws prohibiting marriage in the United States." *Journal of the American Medical Association* 209:534-538.

Kunstadter, P.; Buhler, R.; Stephan, F.; and Westoff, C. 1963. "Demographic variability and preferential marriage patterns." *American Journal of Physical Anthropology* 21: 511-519.

Lerner, I. M. 1968. *Heredity, Evolution, and Society.* San Francisco: W. H. Freeman and Company.

McKusick, V. A.; Hostetler, J. A.; Egeland, J. A.; and Eldridge, R. 1964. "The distribution of certain genes in the Old Order Amish." *Cold Spring Harbor Symposium on Quantitative Biology* 29:99-114.

Salzano, F. M.; Neel, J. V.; and Maybury-Lewis, D. 1967. "I. Demographic data on two additional villages: genetic structure of the tribe."*American Journal of Human Genetics* 19: 463-489.

6 | Disease and Natural Selection

The arrival in Guam of ships under the command of Ferdinand Magellan may have been a less dramatic event in the eyes of these Micronesian islanders than Western writers are wont to think, for the islanders had been visited by sailors from Asia and other parts of the Pacific on countless earlier occasions. But the marking of the island on European navigational charts and maps spelled the beginning of a turbulent history of disease and death which forever changed the course of the future for these handsome islanders whom Magellan so ungallantly labeled as thieves. The ports of Guam became havens for brief visits by a variety of European ships in the period after the discovery of the island in 1521, and a regular harbor for ships of the Spanish galleon sailing between Mexico and the Philippine Islands, but visits were brief and contacts cursory until a small Catholic mission was established on the island in 1668.

By 1710, the population of the Mariana Islands, of which Guam is the largest and most southerly island, had declined from perhaps 50,000 natives to less than 4,000 people, and the remaining natives of the Mariana Islands had been concentrated into a few church villages on the islands of Guam and on Rota Island. By 1786, less than 1,500 natives remained, while a mestizo population, formed from the unions of natives with Mexican, Spanish, and Filipino visitors, numbered over 3,000. While the records are incomplete, and identification of specific diseases made impossible by the vagueness of descriptions, at least three major epidemics—in 1688, 1699, and 1779—had played a major role in the decimation of this Micronesian population. Fortunately, the records of population growth and disease incidence in following centuries permit a clearer view of the extent to which epidemic diseases altered the course of the population history of Guam.

According to one observer of nineteenth-century Guam, a ship arrived at Apra Harbor from the Philippine Islands in 1856, and its passengers related that a burial at sea had taken place only the day before reaching Guam. The deceased man, a victim of smallpox, had by then had ample opportunity to infect the remaining voyagers who promptly carried the news, and the causative virus of smallpox, to the hapless inhabitants of Guam. Within nine months, the population of Guam, numbering over 9,000 persons at the beginning of the year, had been reduced by nearly half, and responsible governmental authorities began an intensive program of sponsored immigration, bringing in settlers to the Mariana Islands from the Philippine and Caroline Islands, and, later, from Japan.

Recovery was slow, however, and, by 1897, the year prior to the American occupation of the island, slightly less than 9,000 people resided in Guam. The growth of the Guamanian population was to suffer one more setback as a result of the 1918 influenza pandemic, but the improvement of sanitary conditions and, later, the introduction of modern medical practices, led to a rapid, steadily increasing rate of population growth in Guam during the twentieth century (Figure 6). Understandably, by this time, the genetic composition of the Guamanian population and the cultural traditions of the society had been drastically and irreversibly altered by the effects of disease.

The microcosmic view of the history and effects of disease as seen in the small island of Guam is representative of events which took place in different countries and at different times with similarly long-reaching consequences. Bubonic plague, which is primarily a disease confined to rodent populations, is occasionally transmitted to human hosts by fleas. However, the disease may also develop into a pneumonic form in humans which can be spread directly from human to human, and this mode of transmission was certainly involved in the three great pandemics of the disease recorded in the sixth, fourteenth, and seventeenth centuries. The "Black Death," or bubonic plague pandemic of 1346-1361, killed perhaps twenty-five million people, or about one-fourth of the entire population of Europe at that time. According to historians, the resultant shortage of labor contributed greatly to the decline of the feudal system and, in England, ultimately to the replacement of the old feudal aristocracy by

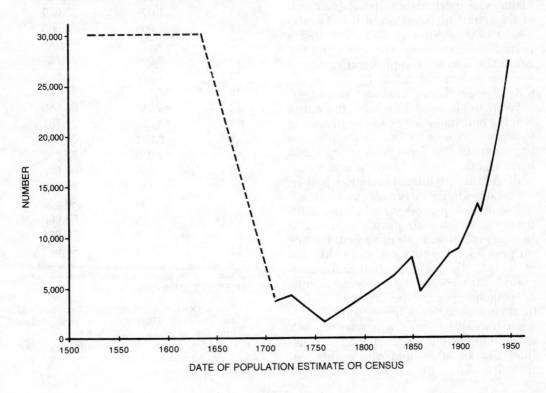

DATE OF POPULATION ESTIMATE OR CENSUS

a new class of farmer land-owners. Smallpox, introduced into Mexico by a slave of the Spanish commander, Narvaez, in 1520, spread through the Indian natives with unparalleled speed and ferocity. When Cortez returned in April 1521, to recapture Mexico City from the rebellious natives, his troops found a city already decimated by this first smallpox epidemic which, according to Ackerknecht, resulted in several million deaths.[1] Syphilis, which some medical historians contend was introduced into Europe by returning members of early expeditions to the New World in the fifteenth century, was apparently far more virulent and contagious in Europe at that time than it is at present. Early descriptions picture bodies covered with ulcerated sores, eroded lips and eyes, and victims wracked with muscular pain and fever. According to Cartwright, Russian history was incalculably altered as a result of the syphilitic infection of Ivan IV, sixteenth czar of Russia, who instigated a period of unremitting repression and terror as the course of syphilis affected his nervous system and induced gross personality changes during his latter years.[2]

We scarcely need to review the entire lengthy and tragic litany of the history of epidemic diseases in human populations to recognize that infectious disease has been a potent factor in the maintenance and patterning of human variation. Rather, we must begin with a broader understanding of disease processes and physical illnesses that have so deeply influenced human evolution. It is convenient for this purpose to recognize a simple division of human illnesses into two main categories—diseases caused by living agents, or pathogenic parasites of man (*infectious diseases*), and *noninfectious diseases* traceable to nonliving agents, such as pathologies due to genetic defects, deficiencies, or other nonbiotic agents. Although useful for the purpose of beginning

to study the effects of disease in human populations, this division is an arbitrary one since interactions between the differ-

TABLE 13
THE MATHEMATICS OF AN IMAGINARY EPIDEMIC IN A POPULATION OF 100,000.

Time (incubation period)	New Cases (number infected = 2)	Total cases (new and old)
0	1	1
1	2	3
2	4	7
3	8	15
4	16	31
5	32	63
6	64	127
7	128	255
8	254	509
9	507	1,016
10	1,004	2,020
11	1,966	3,986
12	3,775	7,761
13	6,966	14,727
14	11,879	26,606
15	17,437	44,043
16	19,515	63,558
17	14,223	77,781
18	6,321	84,102
19	2,010	86,112
20	558	86,670
21	149	86,819
22	39	86,858
23	10	86,868
24	3	86,871
25	1	86,872

Wallace, B. 1972. ESSAYS IN SOCIAL BIOLOGY, vol. III: DISEASE, SEX, COMMUNICATION, BEHAVIOR. Englewood Cliffs: Prentice-Hall, Inc. By permission of the publisher.

1. E. A. Ackerknecht, *History and Geography of the Most Important Diseases* (New York: Hafner Publishing Company, Inc., 1965) p. 63.

2. F. F. Cartwright, *Disease and History* (New York: New American Library, Mentor Book ed., 1972) pp. 69-72.

ent kinds of diseases occur commonly. The victim of the hereditary disease, agammaglobulinemia, lacks resistance to bacterial infection and may die from bacterial infections which produce only mild symptoms in persons lacking the genetic defect. And, of course, the chronically malnourished child may also fail to survive an otherwise mild attack of measles.

Infectious diseases may be further subdivided into those *contagious diseases* in which the causative organism is dependent on man as a sole host and is transmitted by human-to-human contact, and *noncontagious diseases* which cannot normally be spread by person-to-person transmission. Most of us are familiar with such common contagious diseases as chicken pox, mumps, or measles, which are usually mild in their effects in Western peoples, but have often proven highly fatal to native populations when first exposed to these viruses. We are less likely to have firsthand familiarity with such noncontagious infectious diseases as bubonic plague or malaria, both of which involve transmission of a causative microorganism by a third animal—rodents in the case of bubonic plague or mosquitos in malaria—or with such contagious, but mainly waterborne diseases as typhoid fever. Occasionally, the form of specific diseases may vary, so that the mode of transmission alters from one involving an intermediate *vector*, or carrier of disease-causing microorganisms, to direct transmission. Thus, three forms of plague are known, of which one can be transmitted by direct contact. As already noted, it is likely that the rapid spread of plague and the involvement of millions during the several pandemics known to have occurred between the sixth and seventeenth centuries necessarily involved a shift from the bubonic, rat-borne, form to the pneumonic form of the disease.

Many factors affect the spread of contagious diseases in exposed human populations, and the outcome of epidemics involves an interaction between such characteristics as the virulence, infectivity, and pathogenicity of the parasite, and the degree of genetic resistance, susceptibility and immunity levels of the host population. A simplified model of the course of an epidemic through a hypothetical population can be developed to provide some insight into the progress of an epidemic through a population all of whose members are susceptible to the infection (Table 13). This model may well provide a close proximation to the course of an epidemic disease in a "virgin population," that is, one without previous exposure to the specific disease-causing organism, with the possible exception of the low value (2) of persons who could be expected to be infected by a person already carrying the disease.

However, the virulence or pathogenicity of the causative organism may be attenuated during passage through human hosts or over time, as seems to have occurred in past years as scarlet fever, an often fatal childhood scourge in this country in the early decades of this century, has assumed a milder form, known today as scarlatina. Moreover, the initial exposure to an epidemic may result in the differential survival of individuals with greater genetic resistance to the disease, or leave behind a population with acquired immunity to subsequent reinfection. In the latter case, as new individuals join the population, through birth or immigration, an increasing proportion of susceptible individuals becomes available for infection at some later date. Conversely, the history of passage through a host population may also result in genetic changes in the parasite population. A highly virulent strain of a pathogenic organism may cause such rapid, extensive mortality in the host population that only those microorganisms producing milder effects survive to be transmitted to other hosts. Such changes in parasitic virulence seem to have been implicated in the reappearance of myxomatosis, a virus disease introduced into the rabbit population of Australia in an effort to control the burgeoning numbers of rabbits in that country. Similarly, the repeated appearances of new, virulent strains of the influenza-A virus in human populations suggests some results of mutual interactions involving genetic changes in host and parasite populations.

Since the spread of contagious infections is influenced by the interaction of human host and parasite, the proportion of susceptible individuals, and the frequency of contact between individuals, sociocultural factors affecting settlement patterns, levels of interpersonal contacts, prevailing notions of sanitation and hygiene, and other conditions affecting the dissemination of pathogenic microorganisms are as critical to the effects of disease on human populations as the basic biological attributes of the host and parasite populations. A common theme running through the disease histories of native populations in North and South America, Australia, and the Pacific turns on the decimating effects of infectious diseases in native populations brought together into dense settlements, either by administrative fiat or in response to the growth of new towns and population centers. Indeed, Fiennes argues that infectious disease as known today in man is a specific consequence of civilization dating from the period when an agricultural economy began to provide the basis for the rise and growth of settled, densely populated communities.[3]

Since, unfortunately, many of the diseases which mankind suffers do not affect the skeleton, there is little direct evidence available in fossil remains of the conditions of disease in ancient populations.

However, knowledge of the requisite conditions for the dissemination and maintenance of infectious microorganisms in human hosts can be used to indicate the probable disease status of human populations during the distant past. It seems likely that early man, living in groups of limited numbers, was not subject to infectious diseases, such as smallpox or measles, which require a rapid transmission of pathogenic organisms by direct human-to-human contact and the availability of a number of susceptible individuals over time adequate to maintain the populations of causative viruses. Diseases involving an intermediate animal vector, such as malaria, would probably have required a minimal level of human host population density to maintain continued transmission of the infective organism and, in any case, could not have been maintained in those parts of the world where the necessary ecological conditions required for the survival of the vector population did not exist. Thus, as many students of the history of disease have claimed, the adoption of a sedentary life based on an agricultural economy must have resulted in a radical shift in the kinds of diseases to which human populations were subject.

Settled human groups, whose larger numbers and greater density could have been maintained by the provision of foodstuffs intentionally grown for consumption, and stored to insure survival during periods of shortages, would have presented better conditions for the survival and persistence of pathogenic organisms requiring minimal levels of host population size for their continued survival through persistent reinfection. Moreover,

3. R. Fiennes, *Man, Nature and Disease* (New York: New American Library, Signet Science Library Book ed., 1964) pp. 16-26.

as we have already seen in the case of malaria in West Africa, the clearing activities of human groups engaged in agricultural pursuits often enhanced the success of populations of pathogenic organisms. Settled life, and the problems of sanitation in settled communities, must certainly have increased the rate of parasitism as the occasion for repeated reinfection and contamination with human wastes increased. The association of humans with domesticated animals in these settlements must have further contributed to this problem and provided a source of new diseases transmitted from these animal companions.

As a result of improved sanitation and medical advances in the fields of immunology, modern man is protected by preventive innoculations from the effects of many of the infectious diseases which formerly killed as many as half of all children born alive before reaching adulthood. The discovery of antibiotics and anesthetics, as well as major advances in surgical techniques, have greatly increased the life expectancy of human beings in populations where modern medical facilities are available. The major causes of mortality in populations of developed countries have changed drastically since the beginning of this century, with stress-related heart diseases and cancer assuming a primary role (Table 14).

Although many of the contagious diseases known to modern man have been brought under control in large parts of the world in recent years and will, presumably, be controlled in developing countries in the near future, human populations continued to be exposed to different kinds of *zoonoses*, diseases involving transmission of infections of other animals to humans. Schistosomiasis, filariasis, and malaria are diseases of the tropics and subtropics which do not appear in all areas of the world, but have played an important role

in the evolution of affected populations. Moreover, the genetic consequences of previous disease exposures may continue to be expressed in the form of human differences.

TABLE 14

TEN LEADING CAUSES OF DEATH IN THE UNITED STATES: 1900 and 1967

1900	Deaths per 100,000 Persons	% of All Deaths
1. Pneumonia and influenza	202	11.8
2. Tuberculosis	194	11.3
3. Diarrhea and enteritis	143	8.3
4. Diseases of the heart	137	8.0
5. Cerebral hemorrhage	107	6.2
6. Nephritis	89	5.2
7. Accidents	72	4.2
8. Cancer	64	3.7
9. Diphtheria	40	2.3
10. Meningitis	34	2.0
1967		
1. Diseases of the heart	365	39.0
2. Cancer	157	16.8
3. Cerebral hemorrhage	102	10.9
4. Accidents	57	6.1
5. Pneumonia and influenza	29	3.1
6. Certain diseases of early infancy	24	2.6
7. General arteriosclerosis	19	2.0
8. Diabetes mellitus	18	1.9
9. Other diseases of the circulatory system	15	1.6
10. Emphysema and related diseases	15	1.6

Wallace, B. 1972. ESSAYS IN SOCIAL BIOLOGY, vol. III: DISEASE, SEX, COMMUNICATION, BEHAVIOR. Englewood Cliffs: Prentice-Hall, Inc. By permission of the publisher.

Tay-Sachs disease, also known as infantile amaurotic idiocy, is an hereditary disease, in which the affected child with a homozygous recessive genotype usually dies during the first few years of life. The disease occurs far more frequently among Jews (1 in 6,000 births) than in non-Jews (1 in 500,000 births), suggesting that the allele frequency for this trait is about ten times higher in Ashkenazi Jews than in non-Jews. Studies of the reproductive performance of grandparents of affected children suggest that the Jewish heterozygote has an enhanced reproductive advantage over homozygous normal grandparents, and that the offspring of heterozygote grandparents exhibit enhanced rates of survival to age twenty-one. Aronson has also suggested that the high frequencies of the allele may have resulted from the differential fitness of heterozygotes living in the ghettos of Eastern Europe and subject to typhoid infections.[4]

Similarly, the present-day distributions of the ABO blood groups in human populations may reflect, in part, the outcome of different disease histories. Vogel and Chakravartti, for example, have shown that the relative incidence, severity, and mortality from smallpox are higher in patients with blood groups A and AB than in individuals of blood type B or O.[5] Statistical analyses of hospital data have also revealed an increased incidence of influenza A-2 infections in O-blood type individuals, and of rheumatic fever in persons with A-blood type. Associations between the ABO blood group system and other illnesses, such as various forms of ulcers, have been repeatedly demonstrated. Thus, it seems likely that a number of characteristic blood group allele frequencies of specific human populations may be traced to the direct or indirect consequences of different disease histories.

Amyotrophic lateral sclerosis (ALS), which is more familiarly known as "Lou Gehrig's disease," is a debilitating and progressive form of muscular atrophy following the degeneration of nerve cells in the brain stem and spinal cord, and usually proves fatal within a few years of the first appearance of overt symptoms. The incidence of the disease among the inhabitants of Guam (and of Kure, Japan) is 100 times higher than in other parts of the world, and nearly 10 percent of all adult deaths in Guam were attributable to the disease until very recently. However, in the last few years, no new cases have appeared, suggesting that the causative agent may no longer be operating. Various theories have been proposed to explain the causes of ALS but extensive investigations among natives living in Guam and their relatives living off the island have failed to demonstrate any common environmental factor which might prove a causative or precipitating factor. It has been claimed that the disease, which appears only in mature adults, is due to an autosomal dominant allele which attained high frequencies during the period of severe population size reductions ("bottlenecks") in the seventeenth through nineteenth centuries. As no new cases have appeared on Guam during the last few years, some more sophisticated explanations are due. It seems reasonable to suspect that the disease in Guam may be the secondary result of disease exposure at some earlier date, much as has been claimed for the recent increase around the world in Parkinson's disease in now-mature adults who survived the 1918 influenza pandemic.

However reasonable it is to suspect that genetic resistance to specific diseases takes place through the differential survivorship of more resistant hosts, it is often

4. S. M. Aranson, "Epidemiology," in *Tay-Sachs' Disease*, B. W. Volk, ed. (New York: Grune and Stratton, 1964), pp. 118-154.

5. F. Bogel and M. Chakravartti, "ABO blood groups and smallpox in a rural population of West Bengal and Bihar (India)," *Humangenetik* 3 (1966): 166-180.

difficult to demonstrate unequivocally that natural selection has led to the establishment of a more benign host-parasite relationship through genetic coadaptation. The severe manifestations of such diseases as smallpox or measles in many unexposed native populations was often a source of amazement to European colonizers who, like many of their ancestors, had successfully survived the diseases in relatively mild forms as children. It seems clear, too, that sickle-trait heterozygotes experience a milder form of malarial infestation than individuals with normal hemoglobin, while natives of regions where yellow fever is endemic appear to have natural immunity to the disease. In other cases, it is unclear if a genetic resistance to specific disease conditions is at all responsible for differential disease incidences. The incidence of skin cancer is exceptionally high among Anglos living in some of the southwestern parts of the United States, but Indian populations in the same regions have a much lower incidence of the condition. It is tempting to ascribe the difference in skin cancer incidence to a higher degree of genetic resistance among the Indians who have inhabited these regions for lengthy periods, but a number of cultural differences, including esthetic standards and behavioral practices, also distinguish Indians from their more fair-colored neighbors. Indians of this region place little value on the active acquisition of a sun-bronzed complexion, and certainly do not intentionally seek exposure of large parts of the body to the sun's rays. Similarly, differences in the incidences of such conditions as gallbladder diseases, various forms of cancer, liver diseases, etc., in the different ethnic groups of Hawaii cannot readily be isolated from the numerous microenvironmental differences, including dietary distinctions, which characterize the various groups.

Disease, as we have seen in this hasty review, not only affects the cultural history, but also the genetic composition and biological history, or evolution, of human populations. The major epidemic diseases of mankind, which have so greatly altered the course of recent human history, were probably unknown to human populations prior to the adoption of a settled life in agricultural communities. It seems reasonable to suggest that the major modes of population control (infanticide, abortion, prolonged sexual abstinence) observed in modern groups of hunters and gatherers were employed by most early human groups and, together with high rates of mortality associated with childbearing and the effects of gastrointestinal disorders and respiratory afflictions among infants and toddlers, effectively suppressed rapid population growth. With the advent of an agricultural economy, more densely populated settled communities of humans would have proven more susceptible to the effects of infectious disease as a primary means of population control. The appearance of improved means of transportation and communication between settlements and, later, with different parts of the world, ensured the widespread dissemination of most contagious diseases to all human populations, although zoonoses would have continued to be limited to those populations inhabiting regions where affected animal populations of alternate hosts and of vectors could survive.

In many cases of prolonged exposure to infectious diseases, some degree of host-parasite coadaptation seems to have taken place so that populations differ today in susceptibility as a result of different disease histories. Moreover, genetic differences in traits other than those directly related to specific disease susceptibility characterize modern human populations as a result of different disease histories and in some cases, involves the regrowth of populations once decimated by epidemic diseases.

In highly industrialized countries, recent advances in medical knowledge and skills have effectively reduced the selective intensities posed in the past by many infectious diseases. Stress related diseases and cancer have now assumed the role of primary causes of mortality in these areas. Medical advances have also made the continued survival and reproduction of genetically afflicted individuals more likely and, thus, contributed to new levels of deleterious mutations present in these populations. The advent of modern technology which permits us to operationalize values concerning the intrinsic merit of human life has, directly and indirectly, contributed to the maintenance and patterning of human variation.

For Further Reading

Alland, A. *Adaptation in Cultural Evolution. An Approach to Medical Anthropology.* New York: Columbia University Press, 1970. An introduction to the field of medical anthropology and to the productive relationships of medical and ethnological research.

Cockburn, T. A. "Infectious diseases in ancient populations." *Current Anthropology* 12 (1971):45-62. Summary of major issues and findings of paleopathological research.

Ford, J. "Interactions between human societies and various trypanosome-tsetse-wild fauna complexes." In *Human Ecology in the Tropics.* Edited by J. P. Garlick and R. W. J. Keay, pp. 81-98. Symposia of the Society for the Study of Human Biology, vol. 9. New York: Pergamon Press, 1970. Review of the com-

plex ecological interrelationships of animal and human populations underlying several critical animal-borne diseases affecting African populations.

McDermott, W.; Deuschle, K. W.; and Barnett, C. R. "Health care experiment at Many Farms." *Science* 175 (1972):23-31. Summary report of the results of a planned program of medical improvement in a North American Indian community, with some surprising conclusions.

Otten, C. M. "On pestilence, diet, natural selection, and the distribution of microbial and human blood group antigens and antibodies." *Current Anthropology* 8 (1967): 209-226. Inclusive and provocative summary of pertinent literature and theoretical directions in the study of diet-disease interactions influencing human evolution.

Zinsser, H. *Rats, Lice, and History.* 4th ed. London: George Routledge, 1942. An eminently readable classic of medical history.

Bibliography

Myrianthopoulos, N. C. and Aronson, S. M. 1966. "Population dynamics of Tay-Sachs disease. I. Reproductive fitness and selection." *American Journal of Human Genetics* 18:313-327.

Schreiber, M. M. 1971. "The incidence of skin cancer in southern Arizona (Tucson)." *Archives of Dermatology* 104:124-127.

Wallace, Bruce. 1972. *Essays in Social Biology,* vol. 3: *Disease, Sex, Communication, Behavior.* Englewood Cliffs, N.J.: Prentice-Hall, Inc.

7 | Ode to the Uncommon Man

The diversity which each of us can observe among our fellows is the product and the necessary condition of evolution operating on human populations, past and present. The models we employ to study how evolutionary processes operate to create and maintain variation are highly simplified reductions of complex phenomena which permit us, at best, to suggest approximations of complex processes in reality. Human variation is not fully explained by the Hardy-Weinberg equation and its derivatives any more than the complex relationships and transactions between and among populations of different species in an ecosystem can be totally comprehended in a systems analysis of black boxes and flowcharts. But these, and related models, whether concerned with the dynamics of population growth or the spread of communicable diseases, can provide foundations for understanding complex phenomena by comparisons to predicted outcomes of simplified interactions.

The basic principles of Mendelian and population genetics reveal the immense biological variability present in modern human populations. The availability of vast amounts of genetic variation within the species, and the potential reservoir of unique combinations of genetic materials possible through recombination, provide a potential for genetic adaptation of popula-tions to a wide range of environmental niches. But man's genetic heritage has also provided the biological underpinning for a unique complex of nongenetic responses to environmental stresses through extra-somatic, or cultural, means. The Cahuilla Indians of California have not evolved unique digestive systems for rendering the common acorn digestible, but, instead, have developed complex techniques of soaking and grinding acorns to remove toxic elements from the nut which forms an important part of the native diet. Eskimos have devised highly protective clothing to wear in the Arctic regions while populations of other animal species in Arctic areas exhibit highly specialized modes of genetic adaptations suitable to survival in that climatic zone.

The cultural dimension of human life is not merely an alternative to biological processes, elevating man above their operation, but a novel form of direct influence on biological evolution. The ability to prepare otherwise inedible foodstuffs for safe human consumption obviates genetic or natural selection in favor of those few mutants who might have an essential enzyme required for the utilization of the unmodified form of the item. But the consumption of a newly utilizable food source can provide the necessary economic support for population growth and settled life which, in turn, influences the kinds and intensities of disease pressures affecting the population. Mating practices and patterns can directly affect the rate of inbreeding in different societies, thus altering the efficiency of natural selection operating in different human populations. The control of communicable disease through modern medical knowledge and technology has already altered the characteristic demographic structure of populations in the industrialized nations of the world. Recent changes in ritualistic practices among the Fore natives of New Guinea have produced a radical decrease in the incidence of the kuru disease which once decimated these people.

While it is often practically useful to artifically distinguish biological and cultural factors in analyzing human variation, there is an interplay between the two kinds of phenomena which compounds the effects of either dimension in maintaining and patterning human variation. It is the synergistic, or compounding, effect of biocultural interactions which distinguishes human evolution as unique. Just as variation in any plant or animal species cannot be understood solely in terms of chemical bonding of the DNA molecule, reductionism applied to the interpretation of human diversity proves inadequate to full appreciation of the realities of biological change through time. This text has attempted to focus on biocultural interactions influencing human diversity at the population level as the most inclusive, comprehensive approach available for understanding the meaning of human evolution.

In terms of distribution throughout the world and ability to modify the environment, our species has achieved an unparalleled degree of biological success. Unlike most other species, this has entailed the retention of a high level of phenotypic generalization and diversity. The retention of genetic diversity, made possible in large measure through biocultural differences among different human populations, ensures the likelihood that some populations, at least, would survive under the most radical environmental changes in the future which can be envisioned. In a long-term evolutionary perspective, diversity is the finest insurance policy available to any species. It follows from this perspective that any great reduction in biological or cultural diversity diminishes mankind, not only esthetically, but practically in terms of survival of the species. Cultural plurality is not only a desirable social goal, but a biological necessity.

Glossary

Affines—persons related through marital bonds.

Age-Specific Rates—vital rates of specific age-groups.

Allele—alternative forms of a gene at a single locus.

Autosomal Chromosomes—all chromosomes except the sex (X and Y) chromosomes.

Biotic Potential—the inherent biological capacity for population growth.

Birth Cohort—group of all those individuals born during a specified period of time.

Chief Effect—form of selective mating involving the socially-conferred reproductive advantage of group leaders; reported from the Yąnomamö Indians of South America.

Coefficient of Inbreeding (F)—measure of the probability that two alleles at a locus are identical by descent from a common ancestor.

Cognized Environment—the limited range of biotic and physical environmental potential consistent with prevailing ideas, attitudes, and values of the human population utilizing the resources of a region.

Collateral Relatives—consanguines not related in a direct line of descent (example: siblings).

Consanguineous Relatives—genetically related individuals.

Contagious Disease—infectious diseases involving causative organisms specific to human hosts and transmissible by direct (human-to-human) contact.

Cross-Cousin Marriage—marriage between individuals whose related parents are siblings of unlike sex.

Deme—localized breeding population.

Demography—mathematical and statistical studies of population size, distribution, composition, and changes.

Diploid—2N chromosome number of most body (somatic) cells, numbering forty-six in humans.

Dominant—an allele which is expressed in the phenotype when present in homozygous (DD) or heterozygous (Dd) combination.

Ecological Niche—refers to the functional role of an organism or population of organisms within an ecosystem.

Ecology—the study of the relationships among and between organisms and with their environment.

Endogamy—marital customs requiring marriage within a specified social group.

65

Exogamy—traditions requiring marriage outside of specified social groups.

Fecundity—biological capacity, or potential, for reproduction.

Founder Effect—variations in allele frequencies of small founding samples from a larger ancestral population.

Gametes—sex cells (female ovum and male spermatozoan).

Gene Flow—exchange of genes between populations.

Genetic Drift—variance in allele frequencies as a result of gametic sampling between generations.

Genetotrophic Adaptation—allele frequency changes due to evolutionary adaptations of populations to differing dietary environments.

Genotype—the genetic constitution of the individual.

Genotypic Assortative Mating (Inbreeding)—mating between genetically related individuals.

Haploid—refers to the chromosomal constitution of the mature gamete, numbering twenty-three chromosomes in humans.

Heterogamy—phenotypic negative assortative mating; mating between persons with dissimilar phenotypic traits.

Heterozygote Advantage—differential survivorship or reproductive success of the heterozygote where selection operates against both homozygotes.

Heterozygous—having non-identical alleles of a gene at the same chromosomal locus (example: Dd).

Homogamy—phenotypic positive assortative mating; mating between persons with similar phenotypic traits.

Homozygote Selection—selection against one allele at a locus, by removing the allele when it is expressed in the homozygous (DD or dd) condition.

Homozygous—having identical alleles at the same chromosomal locus.

Hypocaloric Diet—a diet inadequate in total amounts of calories.

Hypoglycemia—low blood sugar level.

Inbreeding—matings between consanguineous relatives; genotypic assortative matings.

Incest—mating or marriage between persons belonging to a culturally defined kinship group within which such relationships are prohibited.

Infectious Diseases—diseases caused by living agents, or pathogenic parasites of man.

Levirate—marriage of a woman to her husband's brother; usually involves the marriage of a widow to her deceased husband's brother.

Life Table—table indicating the probable number of survivors from a birth cohort to each successive age group based on a specific set of death rates for each age category.

Limiting Factors—those essential factors which singly, or in interaction with other elements, are essential to the organism's survival and reproduction.

Lineal Relatives—consanguines related in a direct line of descent (example, parent and offspring).

Locus—site on a chromosome occupied by a gene (plural: loci).

Meiosis—process of reduction-division in the formation of gametes.

Mendelian Population—group of interbreeding individuals that shares a common gene pool.

Mitosis—process of somatic cell replication.

Monozygotic Twins—genetically identical individuals derived from the splitting of a single zygote at an early stage of embryonic development.

Mutation—changes in the structure, composition, or arrangement of the genetic material.

Natural Selection—the differential contribution of specific genotypes to the gene pool of succeeding generations.

Non-Contagious Diseases—infectious diseases which cannot normally be spread by person-to-person (direct) contact.

Non-Infectious Diseases—diseases traceable to nonliving causative agents.

Panmixia—condition of random mating.

Parallel Cousin Marriage—marriage between individuals whose related parents are siblings of the same sex.

Pedigree Inbreeding—the preferential mating of genetic relatives in accordance with prevailing cultural prescriptions.

Phenotypic Polymorphism—intrapopulation (individual) variation in phenotypic traits.

Phenotypic Traits—detectable expressions of the genetic composition of an individual.

Polygenic Trait—trait determined by the cumulative effects of many genes (example: stature).

Polygyny—the marriage of a male to two or more wives simultaneously.

Polytypism—interpopulation variation.

Population Inbreeding—matings of genetically related individuals which are the consequence of limited population size.

Population Pyramid—diagrammatic representation of the age and sex composition of a population at a specific time.

Propositus—affected individual in a pedigree whose discovery leads to the collection of pedigree data.

Recessive—an allele which is expressed in the phenotype only when present in homozygous (dd) combination.

Selective Mating—differential mating opportunities and success of individuals or groups within a society who are deemed preferential mates in terms of their greater degree of adherence to cultural norms.

Sex Chromosomes—sex determining chromosomes X and Y.

Sororate—marriage of a man to his wife's sister(s).

Stationary Population—a stable population which is not changing in size.

Synergistic Effect—compounding effect due to the interactions of two or more factors on a common phenomenon or process.

Vector—organism capable of transmitting pathogenic organisms between species or between members of a population.

Vital Rates—mathematical expression of the relationship of the number of vital events (births, deaths, migrations) to some other number, such as total population size.

Zoonoses—animal diseases which can be transmitted to humans.

Zygote—fertilized egg cell.

Index